HOPE IN THE RUBBLE

A Life Transformed by War and Compassion

BRUNO

Hope in the Rubble

© 2024 Cosmic Group

All rights reserved. No part of this publication may be reproduced, distributed, or transmitted in any form or by any means, including photocopying, recording, or other electronic or mechanical methods, without the prior written permission of the publisher, except in the case of brief quotations embodied in critical reviews and certain other non-commercial uses permitted by copyright law. For permission requests, address inquiries to the publisher.

Cosmic Group

https://www.cosmicgroup.solutions/

This book is a work of non-fiction. All events depicted are real and based on true occurrences. Some names have been retained in their original form, while others have been altered to ensure the privacy and protection of the individuals involved.

First Edition: June, 2024

Dedication

This book is dedicated to the unsung heroes—those extraordinary individuals who toil tirelessly in the shadows, driven not by the allure of recognition, but by an unwavering, bone-deep commitment to alleviating the suffering of their fellow human beings.

To the humanitarian aid workers who willingly leave behind the warm embrace of home and loved ones, venturing boldly into the heart of chaos, into the very crucibles of war and devastation, to bring the light of hope and mercy to those drowning in the depths of violence and despair. They are the angels who walk among us, the beacons of compassion that pierce the suffocating fog of war.

To the brave, beautiful souls who made the ultimate sacrifice— Saifeddin Abutaha, Lalzawmi (Zomi) Frankcom, Damian Soból, Jacob Flickinger, John Chapman, James Henderson, James Kirby, and the countless, nameless others who laid down their lives in service of the world's most vulnerable, the forgotten and the forsaken. Their spirits live on, forever etched in the hearts of those they touched, those they saved, those they granted the precious gift of hope amidst the ruins of shattered lives.

To the awe-inspiring medical professionals of Gaza—the doctors, nurses, paramedics, and support staff who embodied the very essence of heroism, who stood tall and unyielding at their posts even as the world around them crumbled beneath the relentless onslaught of bombs and bullets. They who shielded the innocent with their own bodies when no other shelter remained, who held the hands of the dying and whispered words of comfort even as their own hearts bled with the pain of countless losses.

To the courageous, indomitable journalists of Gaza who paid the ultimate price while bearing witness to the triumph of the human spirit amidst unspeakable violence and devastation. This book stands as a tribute to your sacrifice, a solemn vow to carry forward the truth you gave everything to unveil, to ensure that your legacy will never be forgotten, that your voices will echo through the ages.

To Hind Rajab and the over 15,000 Palestinian children whose young lives were brutally cut short by the unrelenting, merciless gears of this ceaseless conflict. Your souls cry out from the depths of our collective conscience, an anguished indictment of the world's apathy, a brutal reminder of the innocence lost, the futures stolen, the dreams forever shattered upon the altar of war.

To every single person around the globe who refuses to look away, who stands tall in the face of injustice, brutality, and the oppression of the innocent—you who speak truth to power with unwavering moral conviction, who raise your voices in a chorus of outrage and demand for change, who bear witness to the pain of others and refuse to let it go unheard, unseen, unacknowledged.

To the resilient, unconquerable people of Palestine, both those who endure the suffocating grip of occupation and those scattered across the diaspora, carrying the scars of exile engraved upon your hearts. You who have faced decades of dehumanization, of erasure, of the world's indifference to your plight, and yet still dare to dream, to hope, to cling fiercely to your dignity and to the unwavering belief in the possibility of peace.

This work is a testament to the incredible resilience of the human spirit, an ode to the light that refuses to be extinguished even in the deepest, darkest hours of despair. It is a reminder that love, compassion, and the bonds of our shared humanity have the power to ultimately triumph over hatred, violence, and inhumanity—if only we have the courage to embrace these virtues as the inalienable rights of every man, woman, and child on this Earth.

To all of you, I dedicate this humble offering, this attempt to give voice to the voiceless, to honor the strength and sacrifice of those who have given so much in the name of a better world. May these words serve as a beacon of hope, a rallying cry for justice, and evidence of the unbreakable spirit that resides within us all.

Contents

Before We Begin	ix
1. A Flickering Flame	1
2. A Lifeline in the Storm	9
3. The Dust and Dread of Gaza	18
4. Echoes of the Unheard	33
5. The Fragile Sanctuary	45
6. A Haven Blooms	60
7. Into the Mouth of Oblivion	74
8. Choices and Sacrifices	83
9. Endings and Beginnings	93
10. The Weight of Hope	100
Afterword	111

Before We Begin

A Personal Note and Heartfelt Thanks

I never intended to write this book. As an aid worker, my sole focus had always been on providing immediate relief and support to those caught in the crosshairs of war. But as the days turned into weeks, and the weeks into months, I found myself bearing witness to a reality that I could no longer keep confined within the boundaries of my own heart.

With each passing moment in Gaza, I saw the human cost of conflict carved into the faces of the innocent, the echoes of their pain reverberating through the rubble-strewn streets. I held the hands of mothers who had lost their children, of children who had lost their homes, and of families torn apart by the relentless tide of violence. In the midst of this chaos, I realized my silence was no longer an option. The stories of those I met, the resilience and courage I witnessed in the face of unimaginable adversity, demanded to be told. They deserved to be more than mere statistics, more than footnotes in the annals of history.

Before We Begin

And so, I began to write. Not for personal acclaim or recognition, but for the countless lives shattered by this conflict. For the children who may never know the simple joys of a carefree childhood, for the women and men who dream of a future free from the constant specter of fear and uncertainty. Through these pages, I hope to provide a window into the reality on the ground, to give voice to those who have been silenced by the deafening roar of bombs and gunfire. I write in the hope that by bearing witness to their stories, we may all be moved to action, to stand in solidarity with those who have lost so much, and to work towards a future where no child has to grow up in the shadow of war.

This book is a validation of the invincible human spirit, a reminder that even in the darkest of times, hope and compassion can light the way forward. It is a call to action, a plea for us all to recognize our shared humanity and to strive for a world where peace and justice reign supreme.

First and foremost, I express my deepest gratitude to the people of Gaza, whose bravery and resilience in the face of unimaginable adversity left me humbled and forever changed. Your strength is evidence of the unwavering power of the human spirit. To my fellow aid workers, the doctors, nurses, and volunteers who worked tirelessly to bring hope and healing: your dedication, compassion, and selflessness are a shining light in a world too often dimmed by darkness. I am honored to have stood beside you and will carry the memory of your courage always.

I am deeply indebted to my family, friends, and the countless individuals who shared their stories, expertise, or engaged in meaningful dialogue about the issues raised within these pages. Your contributions have enriched this book immeasurably, and I am grateful for every conversation, insight, and act of kindness.

Finally, I offer my deepest thanks to you, dear reader. By opening your heart and mind to the stories contained within these pages, you have become an integral part of this journey. Your empathy, compassion, and willingness to bear witness to the struggles and triumphs of those touched by war are a powerful force for change.

As you read these words, I ask that you further expand your heart to include these stories, and you allow yourself to be moved by the pain and the triumphs, the sorrow and the joy. For it is only by understanding the true cost of war that we can begin to build a path towards lasting peace. It is my hope that these stories will stay with you long after you have turned the final page, inspiring you to join the chorus of voices calling for peace, justice, and understanding in our world.

1

A Flickering Flame

The Call to Action

Bruno sank further into the plush embrace of his Tokyo hotel armchair. The window offered a panoramic view of the city, a kaleidoscope of neon signs pulsing with vibrant energy. It was a stark contrast to the turmoil erupting on the television screen before him. Images of war in Gaza flickered across the flat surface: bodies piled high, a makeshift press conference with harried doctors and hospital staff as a backdrop. This wasn't a scene Bruno was used to witnessing. While he was here in his temporary Tokyo haven, bombs rained relentlessly on Gaza, a world away. Years of globetrotting for various projects had become his routine, a life defined by short-term residences and fleeting encounters. Yet, the allure of new destinations couldn't extinguish the pang of helplessness that clawed at him. Despite the distance, the raw terror chiseled on the faces on the screen affected him deeply, a stark reminder of the suffering far beyond his comfortable sanctuary.

A familiar dread coiled in Bruno's stomach, a constant

serpent slithering through his years in war zones. Though the screen displayed a bombed-out marketplace, foreign in a physical sense, it felt hauntingly familiar. Countless images—social media feeds, news reports, documentaries—had created a mosaic of Gaza City in his mind, etching its vibrant pulse into his memory. He'd felt a connection, a yearning for its life-force, even from the sterile safety of his Tokyo Hotel. Now, in ruins, the Gaza market mirrored the hollowness gnawing at him, a void that had grown ever since...

His mind drifted, unearthing a bittersweet memory, sharp with the tang of grief. Years of crisscrossing the globe, offering his expertise in humanity's most desperate corners. War zones, refugee camps, disaster sites—these were his temporary worksites, filled with the cries of the suffering and the steadfast spirit of human resilience. Amidst the chaos, he'd found purpose, a fire that fueled his every step. It wasn't just a job; it was a calling, a way to mend the emptiness within.

Gazing at the ravaged marketplace, a primal urge surged through Bruno. This sterile cocoon, this life of routine, felt suffocating. He belonged there instead, amidst the dust and the screams, a part of the human tapestry woven from resilience and fear. A deep yearning, a call resonating from his soul, propelled him forward. With newfound resolve etched on his face, Bruno knew his path.

The reporter's voice, a monotone drone against the backdrop of chaos, spoke of civilian casualties, families scattered like dust on the wind, a relentless siege with no foreseeable end. Here, in vibrant Tokyo, the horror unfolded on a screen, muted and distant.

Yet, the images branded themselves onto his memory. The vacant eyes of a young boy, his face marred by ash, mirrored the haunted gaze of a refugee Bruno had met years ago in war-torn Africa. No older than eight, the boy clung to life like a wisp of smoke. Trauma carved a story on his face, deeper than any words. Bruno learned the boy's village had been destroyed, his family's home reduced to ashes in an instant. The boy clutched a tattered photograph, the only thread tethering him to his past. The hollowness in his eyes reflected the emptiness within Bruno, a void born not of war, but of a different kind of loss.

Bruno wasn't a soldier or a politician. He was just Bruno, an ordinary man with an extraordinary passion for helping others. His studies and career had carved a niche in crisis management and health and safety. His day job, though glamorous, wasn't his passion or purpose. He wasn't just the guy ensuring the safety of actors and film crews on movie sets, hopping continents for the next big shoot. He was a health and safety manager, risk assessment consultant—a fun job that brought him face-to-face with fascinating people and breathtaking locations. From luxury film sets to challenging projects, Bruno loved the details, the responsibility of safeguarding lives and work environments. He was thriving, splitting his time between the bustling energy of London and the serene beauty of Beaulieu-sur-Mer, a French Riviera village nestled by the sea. Cobblestone streets winding through the village center led to charming cafes with terraces filled with pots of colorful flowers, perfect for watching the world go by. The air hummed with the lazy buzz of cicadas, a constant soundtrack to the slow pace of life. Here, on sunny days, the scent of saltwater and sunscreen mingled with the aroma of freshly baked bread wafting from local boulangeries. In the distance, the dramatic silhouette of the Maritime Alps added a touch of grandeur to the scene.

But beneath the surface, a different kind of calling

simmered—a secret most wouldn't suspect. Bruno yearned to contribute something real, something beyond the make-believe worlds he helped create. So, whenever a window opened between projects, he volunteered his expertise in the most desperate corners of the world—war-torn regions and disaster zones ravaged by nature's fury. It was in these desolate landscapes that Bruno truly found his purpose. His passion morphed into action, his logistics and security skills becoming weapons to battle suffering.

Days melted into weeks as his Japan-based project unfolded. Tokyo, Nagoya, Kanazawa—each city a vibrant collection of sights, sounds, and delicious food. His work gave him a sense of fulfilment humming beneath the surface. Then, the news from Gaza exploded, shattering his tranquility. The food became tasteless, the joy of discovery replaced by a gnawing worry that overshadowed everything.

Night after night, the news was a relentless assault. Bruno couldn't tear himself away, the images burned into his retinas like searing brands. One scene, in particular, played on a loop in his mind. A frantic mother, her face white with terror, weaved through the chaotic hospital ward. Her voice, a trembling rasp, cut through the din as she described her missing child: "Beautiful, white hair, blonde curls." Each word was a shard of broken glass, piercing the hearts of everyone in the room. She was soon joined by a scrubs-clad doctor who was clearly the child's father. His face, a mask of stoicism cracking at the edges, held a glimmer of desperate hope. Together, they navigated the labyrinthine corridors, their pleas echoing off the sterile walls. Finally, they reached a makeshift triage area—a scene of unimaginable suffering. It was there, amidst the moans of the wounded and the frantic cries of medical personnel, they found him. Their son, still and lifeless, a heartbreaking counterpoint to the chaos surrounding him. The mother's scream, a primal wail of loss, shattered the fragile peace. The father, his own grief threatening to consume him, wrapped his arms around her, a silent promise to hold her together even as he crumbled within. Even the most gifted storyteller, Bruno thought, could never conjure such a scene of raw, unadulterated tragedy. Yet, war, with its cruel indifference, painted these horrifying realities in stark, unforgiving detail.

A wave of nausea rolled through him, churning his stomach and twisting his insides. He shifted restlessly, his gaze darting around the room like a caged animal seeking escape. Just a few more weeks on this project, and then what? The question echoed mercilessly, amplifying his growing panic. He loathed this feeling of powerlessness, the bombed-out marketplace on the screen a constant reminder of Gaza's plight. But could he simply accept it? No. He had to try to help. Even if the odds were stacked impossibly high, he couldn't just stand by. The weight of that daunting reality threatened to suffocate him, but a spark of determination ignited within him, pushing back the darkness.

The devastating news from Gaza spread like wildfire, engulfing not only Bruno's thoughts but also those of his entire circle of friends. The once diverse and vibrant conversations that flowed between them now felt stifled by the unfolding tragedy, every word heavy with the weight of sorrow and disbelief. "When will this madness end?" and "How can the world stand by as innocents suffer?" became the haunting refrains that echoed through their gatherings, a chilling chorus of despair and helplessness.

Among Bruno's friends were those who had seen the ugly face of war firsthand, their military pasts a grim collection of hostile environments and unimaginable horrors. These battle-scarred souls, their eyes haunted by the ghosts of conflicts past, united in their plea for caution. With voices laced with the wisdom of hard-earned experience, they implored Bruno to resist the 'call to action based on his emotional response. The most profound impact, they whispered, their words a solemn prayer, can often be made from a distance, where safety and strategy intertwine.

Bruno understood their concerns, as he himself had navigated the treacherous terrain of war zones on more than one occasion. His friends, with their firsthand knowledge of such environments, knew the potential dangers lurking around every corner. Their caution stemmed from a deep understanding of the consequences of recklessness.

Bruno's former colleague, David, spent a couple of years deployed in the Middle East. David became Bruno's primary source of news beyond the filtered snippets on TV and the often-unreliable social media. Most relevant now, David had been with the first convoy that entered Gaza since the war began after a harsh siege. David's firsthand accounts resonated deeply with Bruno: the escalating crisis, the devastation he witnessed, the desperate need for assistance—it was all far beyond the capacity of any single individual. Yet, the gnawing sense of inaction was intolerable for Bruno.

With the Tokyo project complete, Bruno returned to the south of France. However, what he once called "home" felt different now. The long beach walks, the seafood he loved, all the beauty and glamour—it had all become dull. Even his time spent walking on the ports of Beaulieu or Nice became heavy with worry. All he could do was listen to the news, watching the magical Riviera sunsets while his thoughts remained fixed on the other side of the Mediterranean Sea. There, victims were dying under siege, bombs raining down with brutality displayed live on television. Demonstrations erupted across the globe demanding a ceasefire, but apparently, no one was listening. The pressure wasn't enough to stop the attacks on Gaza.

Another night, the world watched in horror as their television screens flickered with explosions. Bombs rained down on civilians, screams piercing the night, a chaotic symphony of destruction live-streamed into living rooms worldwide. The death count, once a number on a news report, now represented individual lives lost, families shattered. Then, amidst the inferno, the unthinkable happened. A hospital, a refuge in the war-torn landscape, was deliberately targeted in an airstrike. The scene that unfolded was engraved into Bruno's memory forever: a fireball engulfing the building, smoke billowing into the sky, the desperate cries of the wounded mingling with the deafening silence of the dead. Over 500 souls perished that night, hundreds more injured. This wasn't just an attack on a building; it was an assault on the very foundations of humanity, a blatant disregard for human rights and international law. That night, a wave of despair washed over Bruno, a crushing weight that threatened to suffocate him. Yet, amidst the darkness, a hint of defiance emerged. Cities around the world erupted in spontaneous demonstrations. Bruno watched, tears blurring his vision, as thousands upon thousands of voices rose in unison, a chorus of outrage demanding an end to the bloodshed. But the cries for peace fell on deaf ears. The attacks continued, a relentless juggernaut grinding on.

Fueled by a renewed sense of purpose, Bruno saw a window of opportunity. Available now that his project was complete, he snatched his phone, a tremor of urgency coursing through him. His fingers flew across the screen, scrolling through his contacts. Names of aid workers,

NGO representatives, and journalists he'd met during his travels flickered by—familiar faces from war-torn landscapes and desperate refugee camps, all bound by a shared commitment to alleviating suffering. Each call became a desperate plea, a frantic search for any information, any chance to make a difference. "Is there anything I can do to help?" he'd plead, his voice tight with urgency. "Are there any organizations on the ground that need assistance?"

Dead ends were frequent, dashed hopes punctuated by the dial tone. Yet, a few calls offered slivers of hope. A former colleague mentioned a familiar well-respected medical charity in dire need of an emergency management coordinator for their Gaza operation. Bruno knew they were well respected, having worked with them before in Kabul. They were a beacon of medical neutrality in the most dangerous conflict zones. Another contact connected him with a journalist who had just returned from the region, offering a startling firsthand account of the unfolding crisis. The journalist's words painted a nightmarish picture—bombed-out hospitals, overflowing refugee camps, and a population teetering on the brink of starvation.

2

A Lifeline in the Storm

Into the Heart of Conflict

Days blurred together in a relentless cycle of phone calls, frantic emails, and news reports. Bruno clung to the fragile lifeline his contacts had offered, a tenuous connection to the possibility of making a difference. Sleep became a distant luxury. His eyes were constantly glued to the screen, refreshing news feeds for any updates on Gaza. Each sunset brought a fleeting hope that the attacks might cease with the sunrise, or perhaps, he'd finally be assigned a task he could do to help. Social interaction became a forgotten luxury. Instead, Bruno poured his energy into gathering information about the situation on the ground. He devoured news reports from every available source, piecing together a horrifying picture of the devastation in Gaza. He reached out to anyone with firsthand knowledge of the conflict, his network of colleagues and contacts proving invaluable. Every conversation confirmed the desperate need for humanitarian aid, the scale of the crisis far exceeding anything he'd witnessed before.

The subject line of the short, to-the-point email was what he'd been waiting for: "Urgent: Emergency Management Coordinator Needed—Gaza Operation." It continued without preamble: "Following up on our previous collaborations, we're reaching out directly. Given your past work with us and news of your immediate availability, Dr. Nadia, who's spearheading the Gaza operation, is eager to discuss the details. Please contact her directly."

A familiar steeliness settled in Bruno's eyes. War zones weren't uncharted territory for him. He'd traversed some of the world's most volatile regions, his calm demeanor a shield against the chaos that swirled around him. Years of navigating the treacherous landscapes of conflict had honed his instincts to a razor's edge. He knew the flash of fear in a soldier's eyes, the palpable desperation on the faces of civilians caught in the crossfire. He understood the unspoken language of checkpoints and curfews, the weight of suspicion that hung heavy in the air.

Dr. Nadia's voice cracked with raw emotion over the phone line. "Bruno," she began, "Gaza is on the brink. The relentless bombing rains terror down on everything—houses, clinics, schools, markets. Nothing is safe. Just last week, a bomb hit our makeshift clinic in the north. Thankfully, there were no casualties, but it's a constant threat." Her words painted a far more horrifying reality than the news reports could ever convey. Bruno winced, picturing the chaos—the wail of sirens, the screams of the injured, the terrified cries of children.

"We're overwhelmed," Dr. Nadia continued. "The death toll keeps rising—children, women, entire families wiped out in single strikes. The wounded keep pouring in, and our resources are stretched thin. We operate under a constant nightmare of checkpoints, curfews, and airstrikes. But we can't abandon these people. They have nowhere else to go. We're a lifeline, a fragile hope amidst the chaos. That's why your role is so crucial, Bruno. You're our shield, our line of defense against the madness."

The phone call with Dr. Nadia, head of the NGO's Gaza operation, ripped the sterile efficiency of their email exchange to shreds. Her voice, raw with a tremor of fear and laced with a desperate urgency, slammed into Bruno. Hearing about the day to day reality and what he and his team could expect was overwhelming, a brutal awakening to the true horror unfolding in Gaza. As she spoke, a vivid picture seared itself into his mind: bombed-out buildings spewing plumes of smoke, terrified family members clinging to each other amidst the rubble, the wail of sirens a constant, mournful cry. A cold dread, heavy and suffocating, settled in his gut, squeezing the air from his lungs.

Dr. Nadia's voice hitched, a tremor that spoke volumes more than words. "Bruno," she continued, her voice barely a whisper, "the clinic... it's become a refugee camp itself. People are crammed everywhere, overflowing into the hallways, their eyes wide with terror and exhaustion. We have children huddled together for comfort, mothers clutching their infants close, and elderly folks clutching whatever meager possessions they could salvage from the bombings. There's no food, clean water is a luxury, and the electricity cuts plunge us into darkness with every terrifying boom, the silence punctuated only by the whimpers of the wounded and the prayers of the afraid." A raw pain laced her words as she described their struggle. "We're operating by flashlight, Bruno, rationing every bandage, every precious vial of medication. Each decision feels like a life-or-death gamble in this constant fight against time and dwindling resources. The generators splutter and cough, threatening to plunge us back into darkness, and the medical supplies dwindle with each new wave of casualties. It's a desperate situation, Bruno, a microcosm of the suffering engulfing Gaza. We're a lifeline to these people, a fragile thread of hope in a world teetering on the brink."

A powerful surge of determination coursed through Bruno. The news reports and images no longer felt distant. Dr. Nadia's voice, filled with exhaustion and a bit of hope, brought the suffering to life. He knew the dangers, the constant threat of violence, the potential for loss. The raw desperation in her voice resonated deeply. These people had nowhere else to go. This wasn't just another war zone; this was Gaza, her description of the human cost of conflict struck him with a painful familiarity.

Dr. Nadia," Bruno cut in, his voice resolute. "Consider it done. I'll be there as soon as possible."

The following days were a whirlwind of bureaucratic nightmares. Securing a visa for Gaza felt like navigating a minefield blindfolded. Each delay—every form, every pointless phone call—was a fresh stab of frustration. Yet, with each hurdle overcome, Bruno's resolve grew like a callus on his soul. Every delay meant more suffering in Gaza, more lives hanging in the balance. Finally, after a tense week of negotiations and enough paperwork to wallpaper a bunker, the visa arrived—a small but crucial victory.

He couldn't bring himself to tell his family. The worry that would be etched on their faces was not a picture he could bear to paint. But he confided in Ronnie, his closest friend and partner-in-crime on countless missions, both harrowing and hilarious. Ronnie, a seasoned veteran with enough war stories to fill a library (and enough scars to illustrate them), had probably worked in most of the world's dubious vacation spots. He and Bruno had a bond forged in shared danger, a friendship that ran almost as deep as some of the scrapes they'd pulled each other out of.

"Going to Gaza," Bruno said casually, trying to mask the knot of apprehension twisting in his gut. "Emergency management coordinator gig. Looks a bit hairy."

Ronnie, a man who'd stared down death more times than he cared to remember, simply raised an eyebrow, a silent understanding passing between them through the crackle of the video call. "Be careful, mate," he said, his voice gruff with a concern that went deeper than words. "And come back in one piece. Though, honestly, with your luck, that might be asking a bit much."

A wry smile tugged at the corner of Bruno's lips. "Thanks, Ronnie. That's the optimism I crave right now."

Bruno paced in restless anticipation, the news a constant barrage of horrors on the television screen. He awaited his flight date, each passing moment a torment. Then, disaster unfolded live. A journalist, a beacon of bravery amidst the chaos, was broadcasting live from Gaza. The scene around him was a horrifying tableau. Plumes of smoke, thick and black, billowed from the ruins of a nearby building. Twisted metal and shattered concrete, a grim testament to the relentless airstrikes, littered the foreground. The camera panned, revealing the destruction stretching outwards, a landscape of devastation.

Bruno watched, heart hammering in his chest, as another explosion rocked the city. The reporter's words, his voice a stark counterpoint to the surrounding pandemonium, echoed earlier recounts of the human cost of the conflict.

Then, in a moment that shattered the illusion of distance with a deafening crack, the journalist's phone buzzed. He answered, a flash of hope momentarily chasing away the grim lines on his face. But that hope died as quickly as it came. The raw emotions that flooded his features were a brutal tapestry woven with shock, a soul-crushing weight of grief, and a steely resolve struggling to break through. It was a confirmation of the unimaginable loss he had just suffered—his own family were victims of another Israeli airstrike. The world held its breath, a collective gasp of horror erupting in living rooms across the globe. The silence on the airwaves was deafening, broken only by the journalist's ragged breaths. Yet, within the depths of his despair, a burst of defiance emerged. It was a faint ember, but it burned with an unwavering determination. He wouldn't let this break him. He had a mission, a responsibility to bear witness to the suffering, and he would continue. Tears welled in his eyes, a silent scream echoing the agony within him, but his voice, when he finally spoke again, remained steady, a beacon of courage amidst the storm of chaos.

The journalist, once a mere chronicler of tragedy, was now thrust into the spotlight, his own life story becoming the most agonizing headline. Cameras swarmed him, capturing the raw and visceral emotions carved on his face —a mixture of shock, grief, and a bit of defiance. He was forced to become the embodiment of the very suffering he reported, forced to confront the ugliest face of war—the unbearable loss of loved ones.

The world watched, hearts heavy, as the reporter raced through the bombed-out streets, his desperate hope dwindling with each passing moment. The devastating scene unfolded live—his shaking hands reaching for the lifeless bodies of his family, the silence broken only by his choked sobs. A single, heartbreaking image spread across the globe: the reporter, cradling his dead son, whispering a lullaby of comfort—"It's okay, it's okay." Was it faith, bravery, or a primal human instinct to shield his child from the harsh reality? Even the news anchor in the studio, a seasoned professional, struggled to maintain composure, tears glistening in her eyes.

But amidst the crushing despair, a glimmer of resilience emerged. Mere hours later, the reporter stood before the camera once more, his blue press vest a stark contrast to the devastation surrounding him. His voice, though thick with emotion, continued with a quiet strength. He spoke of his family, the love he had lost, the void that would forever scar his soul. Yet, his grief was intertwined with a profound sense of purpose. He spoke of the countless others in Gaza who shared his pain, their stories mirroring his own tragedy. His mission, to bear witness to the human cost of conflict, remained unchanged. The statistics and political noise that often obscured the true face of war would not deter him. He would continue to report the truth, his unwavering commitment proof of the enduring spirit of journalism. In that moment, he wasn't just a reporter; he was a symbol of hope, a beacon of courage in the darkest of times. He was a hero, not the fantastical kind, but a real-life hero who walked among us.

Bruno was haunted by these images, a relentless slideshow of suffering burned into his memory. They weren't just pictures on a screen; they were a harrowing glimpse into the reality he was about to face. It wasn't merely the physical devastation—the bombed-out buildings, the pulverized schools, homes reduced to mountains of rubble. It wasn't just the ever-present threat of violence that hung heavy in the air. It was the emotional wreckage that weighed the heaviest.

Shattered lives. Orphaned children with eyes hollowed by grief. A beautiful little girl, no more than five, her angelic face smudged with dust and ash from the blast.

Rescued from the ruins of her home, she didn't know where her family was. Yet, amidst the unimaginable pain, a flash of resilience. As Bruno watched the footage, he saw her lying on the hospital floor, a heartbreaking smile breaking through her tears. She waved at the camera, a tiny sign of hope in a world drowning in despair.

There were other stories too, raw and unfiltered. Boys barely ten years old, clinging to life in hospital beds, sharing the grim tally of the dead and the living after the strike on their home. One boy, bandaged and bruised, lay beside his injured father, whispering words of comfort. "It's okay," he soothed, the roles reversed, the child calming the adult. These weren't scripted narratives, but the brutal truth of war visited upon innocent civilians. The vacant eyes, the gnawing fear fixed on every face—a testament to the human cost of conflict. This wasn't just another war zone; this was Gaza, a place where the suffering took on a painful familiarity, a place where Bruno knew, deep in his gut, he had to be.

As the departure date loomed closer, casting a long, ominous shadow, a steely resolve hardened in Bruno's gut. He harbored no delusions of being a lone hero, single-handedly fixing Gaza. He was Bruno, a single gear in a vast machine desperately trying to function amidst the unfolding catastrophe. This wasn't a sightseeing excursion; it was a descent into a living hell. He wasn't going as a helpless observer, but as a solitary shield against the relentless storm, a lifeline he fervently prayed wouldn't snap under the weight of a shattered world.

Packing became a grim ritual. Gone were the days of fantasizing about exotic destinations or idyllic beaches for sunbathing and relaxation. Gone were the images of turquoise waters teeming with life, replaced by the horrifying reality of Gaza. The once vibrant sea had become a graveyard for fishing boats and fishermen, their dreams swallowed by the depths. Pristine beaches were now refugee camps overflowing with desperate people struggling to find food and water. Roads, once arteries of commerce, were now mangled wrecks, evidence of the relentless bombing.

Each item that was meticulously chosen and placed in his bag held the weight of a potential life saved, a silent promise whispered in the sterile air of his room. He was preparing for a humanitarian mission, a desperate call to action, to harness his skills, to help others. He was going exactly where he needed to be.

3

The Dust and Dread of Gaza

Gaza's Harsh Realities

Cairo buzzed with a nervous energy as news reports streamed from Gaza. The bombing campaign intensified, each report included the rising death toll. Despite the global unease, a single beacon of hope awaited Bruno at the airport—a representative from the NGO, ready to escort him to the team's temporary hotel. Gaza awaited them the next day.

The hotel bustled with activity. Bruno, with his years of experience, began coordinating logistics—securing permits, charting their route into the volatile Gaza Strip. He knew the wait for permits was a patience game, often ending in last-minute approvals.

Meeting his team was a sobering experience. Doctors and medics, seasoned and new, assembled for introductions. The veterans bore the deep lines of past deployments, their eyes reflecting a quiet understanding. The rookies, a mix of excitement and trepidation on their faces, were about to face their trial by fire. Even the veterans, glued to the news, knew this deployment would be unlike any other.

Bruno led a pre-deployment briefing, drawing on intel from on-the-ground sources, officials, and journalists. His network, activated to smooth their mission, offered a clearer picture of the situation. The mission was simple yet daunting: maximize aid to the injured and displaced. Bruno outlined their specialties—the types of surgeries they could perform. The security briefing was grim—a constant state of war, punctuated by brutality and uncertainty. Emergency procedures would be fluid, adapting to the ever-changing situation. Personal safety was paramount. They would be confined to their designated workspace and accommodation; solo movement was strictly prohibited. Communication, a constant challenge in Gaza, would rely on a mix of radios and a satellite phone for emergencies, as most communication towers lay in ruins.

Documentation and legal matters, though tedious, held a new weight. They were in a war zone, and escalation was a constant threat. Bruno emphasized the need for preparedness.

Despite their anxieties, a spark of determination burned in their eyes. These were people who volunteered for a reason—to help those in need. Bruno, with a touch of wry humor intended to steal them for what lay ahead, dismissed them for some rest—a rare commodity in the days to come.

The next morning, a tense energy buzzed around the team as they assembled outside the hotel. Nervous smiles played on some faces, a mask barely concealing the worry beneath. Dr. Francois, a seasoned veteran of war zones, stood calm amidst the storm. His weathered features and ever-present coffee flask spoke volumes of his experience. A familiar face to Gaza, he had answered the call of duty once more. Beside him, Imane, the veteran nurse, radiated an infectious passion for the mission. Her words shared with colleagues were a balm of encouragement in the face of uncertainty. Bruno, the team leader, remained a focused hub of activity, gathering updates and coordinating communications for the journey ahead.

The team boarded the bus, a collective breath held as they rumbled towards the Egyptian border. The journey stretched for over five hours, punctuated only by sporadic bursts of conversation and the heavy silence of anticipation. Every checkpoint, a hurdle cleared, brought them closer to their destination. Egyptian officials boarded the bus, meticulously checking IDs before waving them on.

As they neared the border, the landscape transformed. A sea of white humanitarian aid trucks emblazoned with UN and international logos lined the dusty road. This was a stark reminder of Gaza's plight. Hundreds of trucks— over 700 in all—baked under the relentless desert sun, overflowing with food, medical supplies, and water—a lifeline desperately needed on the other side of the imposing border walls. Yet, only a trickle, a mere twenty trucks a day, were allowed to cross. Frustration and heartbreak welled within the team. Here, stacked high, were the very resources Gaza craved, yet just beyond reach, millions struggled under siege. The weight of this injustice hung heavy in the air.

They pressed on, the endless line of trucks flanking them until finally, the imposing Rafah border crossing loomed ahead.

Seasoned veterans like Bruno and Dr. Francois scanned their surroundings with a practiced wariness. Their grim expressions matched the oppressive atmosphere at the border crossing. For the younger team members, however, a hint of raw fear replaced the bravado they might have harbored beforehand. Their wide eyes, accustomed only to the sanitized horror of news broadcasts, now reflected the chilling reality unfolding before them.

The Israeli checkpoint was a nerve-wracking ordeal. Heavily armed soldiers, fingers hovering near triggers, guarded the fortified positions. Here, they abandoned the bus for a convoy of white NGO SUVs, each emblazoned with the organization's logo and a defiant flag flapping in the wind. Bruno had already assigned teams to their respective vehicles.

The air felt heavy with suspicion. Every shouted question, lost in the fog of their limited understanding, felt like another attempt to unearth a hidden threat. Bags were meticulously scrutinized, the process bordering on sadistic. The long wait under the relentless sun, punctuated by constant frisks and barked commands, felt like a deliberate gauntlet designed to intimidate and demoralize.

Finally, the ordeal ended. Passports and IDs were returned, and with a curt dismissal, they were allowed to proceed. Their destination—Rafah's largest medical complex—wasn't difficult to find. Coordinators, their faces etched with weariness but their spirits resolute, awaited them, a stark reminder of the overwhelming crisis that consumed Gaza.

As the SUVs rolled into Gaza, the landscape transformed into a wasteland. Buildings lay in skeletal ruins, concrete teeth jutting from the ravaged earth. The stench of burned plastic and sewage hung heavy in the air, a constant assault on the senses. Columns of smoke billowed from distant fires, visible on the horizon from several directions, a grim reminder of the ongoing violence. This wasn't the sterile disaster zone depicted in news reports; this was a living, breathing city under siege, and they were about to become a part of its desperate struggle.

The roar of drone strikes and explosions grew steadily louder with each passing mile. The relentless human tide lining the road highlighted the city's plight. Families trudged on foot, their weary faces scored with lines that spoke of nights spent huddled in shelters, of the ever-present fear for their children's lives. Donkey carts, piled high with salvaged belongings—remnants of shattered homes—were guided through the chaotic flow, signs of the human spirit's ability to remain hopeful of rebuilding a home despite unimaginable hardship. Tents, a sprawling canvas of displacement, stretched as far as the eye could see under the shadow of the bombed-out city. Rafah, once a vibrant city of over 300,000 Palestinians, now housed approximately an additional million people displaced by the violence. The air thrummed with a low hum of human activity, a constant reminder of the lives shattered by the conflict. It was a scene sketched in shades of dust and despair, proof of the enduring strength of a people clinging to hope amidst the ruins.

The hospital itself stood as a defiant monument to the medical staff's tenacity. Yet, the surrounding park had become a sea of weary faces huddled beneath a sprawling canvas of tents. On one side was a cluster of press and journalists, easily identified by their blue helmets, bullet-proof vests, and the glint of microphones and cameras capturing the unfolding horror live. On the other, a scene straight out of a nightmare: bodies sprawled on the ground, some shrouded in white bags, others covered with mere duvets. Around them, a tableau of human grief—some wailing openly, others numb with shock.

The sterile scent of disinfectant, once a hospital's signature, had been usurped by a putrid cocktail of sweat, blood, and burned flesh. The relentless beeping of machines struggled to be heard over the cacophony of moans, shouts, and the frantic barking of orders. Each shrill beep a desperate plea against the rising tide of wounded bodies flooding through the shattered double doors. Bloodstained bandages, like discarded macabre confetti, littered the grimy floor, evidence of the relentless violence that had become this city's grim heartbeat.

Inside the overflowing corridors, shadows danced in the unsteady fluorescent lights. Children, their small bodies dwarfed by oversized hospital gowns, whimpered with unseen injuries. Wide, haunted eyes stared vacantly, reflecting a terror no fairy tale could ever extinguish. Exhausted doctors, their faces etched with lines deeper than any scalpel could carve, barked orders with a raw desperation as the machines struggled to keep their patients tethered to life. The coppery scent of blood hung heavy in the air, a constant reminder that this makeshift sanctuary could be reduced to rubble in the blink of an eye.

Bruno and his team were met by Dr. Nadia, her voice a rasp that spoke volumes of her exhaustion. "Welcome to the madhouse, Bruno," she said, a glimmer of dark humor in her tired eyes.

As Bruno introduced his team to Dr. Nadia, the toll of endless days and sleepless nights was reflected in the many lines on her face. Her voice, once a clear and confident instrument, now emerged as a hoarse whisper, each word a struggle against the exhaustion that threatened to consume her. She ushered them through the labyrinthine corridors of the hospital, navigating the surging tide of displaced humanity that pressed in from all sides.

The air hung heavy, a suffocating mix of the sickly-sweet stench of disinfectant and the nauseating, coppery tang of blood. It clung to their lungs, a constant reminder of the suffering that permeated every corner of this once-pristine facility. As they moved through the throng, haunted eyes turned their way, each gaunt and exhausted face a portrait of worry and despair. In those weary gazes, Bruno saw a silent plea, a desperate cry for help from those teetering on the brink of hopelessness.

A makeshift ward, stripped bare of its former sterility, offered a glimpse of their new reality. Here, the team dropped their bags, the weight of their mission pressing down on them like a physical burden. Dr. Francois, his brow furrowed in a silent vow, clenched his jaw. Imane, the veteran nurse, fought back a sob, a tear tracing a glistening path down her cheek. The younger team members, their faces pale and drawn, looked around with wide, shocked eyes. This wasn't the sterile environment they'd envisioned in training exercises; this was a war zone barely resembling a hospital.

Bruno, ever the pragmatist, began taking notes, his gaze darting across overflowing beds and makeshift IV poles rigged from scavenged materials. The whirring of generators, a constant counterpoint to the moans of the wounded, served as a stark reminder of the hospital's precarious existence.

Dr. Nadia launched into a grim litany. Electricity was a precious commodity, reserved for critical machines like kidney dialysis units. Lifesaving treatments, such as hemodialysis for patients with acute kidney injury (AKI) or renal failure, and ventilator support for patients with acute respiratory distress syndrome (ARDS), were frequently postponed due to fuel shortages, forcing them to make impossible choices about who would live and who would die.

Medical supplies dwindled with each passing day, and even the most basic pain medication, like ibuprofen or acetaminophen, became a luxury. The stench of gangrene hung heavy in the air, without enough antibiotics to prevent infections after surgeries or to treat existing infections. The screams of patients echoing through the halls were a constant reminder of the surgeries that had to be performed without anesthesia.

As they ventured deeper into the heart of the hospital, the weight of the unfolding crisis seemed to press down upon them with every step, an invisible force that threatened to squeeze the very air from their lungs. The relentless misery hung thick in the stale atmosphere, a palpable entity that permeated every corner and crevice, threatening to suffocate them beneath its oppressive shroud.

Yet amidst this landscape of despair, they encountered Dr. Omar, the hospital manager, a beacon of resilience in the face of overwhelming adversity. Though there were deep lines of stress and pain around his eyes, a witness to the unimaginable burdens he shouldered, there burned within him a fierce glimmer of rebellion—a lone ember stubbornly driving him to continue doing his best to save lives amidst the ashes of destruction.

As he extended his hand in greeting, his grip firm and unwavering, Bruno could feel the unspoken plea for help that emanated from every fiber of Dr. Omar's being. A subtle tremor ran through his hand, a silent betrayal of the countless hours of sleep he had willingly sacrificed, the meager meals he had choked down in hasty gulps, all for the sake of keeping this fragile lifeline from fraying beyond repair.

In that moment, as their hands clasped in a gesture of solidarity and shared purpose, Bruno understood the true depths of the dedication and selflessness that drove this extraordinary man. Against all odds, in the face of unimaginable challenges, Dr. Omar had poured every ounce of his strength and determination into maintaining this bastion of hope, this spark of light amidst the encroaching darkness.

"We are in desperate need of any help you can provide," Dr. Omar said, his voice a hoarse whisper, each word scraping against his throat like shards of broken glass, proof of the depths of exhaustion that had seeped into his very bones. "These assaults... they never stop. They come at night, under the cover of darkness, raining down fire and fury upon our people. We treat the wounded, mend the broken, but for every life we save, ten more seem to be lost."

A deep sadness clouded his eyes, a well of unshed tears threatening to overflow. "But we fight on," he continued, his voice gaining strength with each word. "We fight for our patients, for our families, for the very soul of this city. We will not be broken. We will not surrender."

Dr. Omar's words, laced with exhaustion and unwavering determination, struck a chord deep within the team. They had come prepared for hardship, but the sheer scale of the crisis, the relentless cruelty, threatened to overwhelm them. Yet, in Dr. Omar's unwavering spirit, they saw a reflection of their own. They were here to help, to fight alongside these brave medical warriors, to be a ray of hope in the midst of darkness.

The deafening roar of a nearby airstrike cut Dr. Omar's words short. Yet, a spark had ignited in the team's eyes. They knew there would be a lot of challenges to overcome, but the raw desperation in his voice and the sheer scale of the crisis had taken their breath away. Now, a surge of adrenaline coursed through them.

"Let's get to work," Bruno declared, his voice firm and steady.

The team hurried back to the makeshift ward. Donning their scrubs, they shed the weight of their civilian identities and embraced the mantle of medical warriors. Bruno, ever the strategist, delivered a quick briefing. He outlined essential procedures and reiterated the triage protocols based on their initial assessments.

With newfound purpose, they followed Dr. Nadia, their footsteps echoing on the grimy tile floor. Bruno, however, had a different role to play.

He wasted no time. Building an intelligence network became a desperate scramble for survival. He buttonholed weary aid workers, their faces lined with the same haunted dread that mirrored his own growing anxiety. Each conversation was a frantic exchange, punctuated by nervous glances towards the horizon, ever watchful for the next harbinger of destruction. Locals, those stoic souls who hadn't fled or been buried under the rubble, became his lifeline. Hardened by the war but still glowing with a spark of defiance, they were the eyes and ears on the street. Their survival instincts, honed to a razor's edge in this war zone, became his compass, guiding him through the ever shifting dangers.

Training was a grim baptism by fire for Bruno's team. Safety training for medics in this war zone was a dark parody of its intended purpose. How could laminated safety sheets, with their sterile diagrams, possibly prepare these people for the mangled bodies that awaited them? This wasn't a sterile classroom; it was a crash course in survival delivered under the ever present threat of oblivion.

Bruno's words felt hollow as he recounted protocols for shrapnel wounds and triage techniques. The clinic staff, their faces filled with the same haunted dread that matched his own growing anxiety, were already intimately familiar with these realities. Gaza was a place where children learned the boom of an airstrike was the prelude to a terrifying dance—a scramble to find cover, the heart-stopping thud of explosions, the choked cries of those less fortunate. Here, the ground wasn't just the floor; it was a potential bomb shelter, the tremors a disturbing reminder of their precarious existence.

Their terror was a palpable entity, a thick fog clinging to them like the omnipresent dust from the bombings. It choked their lungs and clouded their judgment. Their haunted eyes reflected not just the horrors they'd already witnessed, but the chilling premonition of what was to come. The rhythmic boom of airstrikes wasn't background noise; it was a monstrous drumbeat echoing through the shattered city, a grim counterpoint to the whimpers of the wounded and the frantic shouts of the overworked staff. Each boom was a punctuation mark in the terrifying symphony of destruction, a visceral reminder that staying alive was a matter of blind luck and split-second decisions.

Yet, the most gut-wrenching challenge wasn't the whistle and boom of bombs, a symphony of violence Bruno thought he'd grown accustomed to over the years. Here, the suffering was a tangible entity, a tide threatening to drown them all. A young boy, barely a teenager, lay whimpering on a blood soaked cot. His leg, a mangled mess of bone and flesh, defied any semblance of its original form. Each whimper that escaped his pale lips was a tiny hammer blow to Bruno's chest, a constant reminder of the human cost of this conflict.

An elderly woman, her skin like weathered parchment, sat huddled in a corner, eyes vacant and hollow. Words, when they finally came, tumbled out in a broken whisper—a family, a house, all gone in the blink of an eye. The raw, unfiltered grief hung heavy in the air, a suffocating weight that pressed down on Bruno's soul.

Despite the crushing weight of despair, Bruno plastered a reassuring smile on his face for the staff. His calm facade, a flimsy shield against the ever present dread, was all he had to offer. He was a man playing a part, a Crisis Response Coordinator in a play where the stakes were life and death, and the backdrop was a tapestry woven from the threads of human suffering.

Bruno himself wasn't immune. Previous missions spent in other war zones conditioned him to sleep with his boots on, the rhythmic rise and fall of his own ragged breaths a counterpoint to the distant explosions that rattled the unstable walls. He forced a firm, gentle smile onto his face for the staff. It was a weak barrier against the ever present dread that made it difficult to breathe, a suffocating weight that pressed down on his chest with each labored breath.

But behind the facade, a war of his own raged. The raw, unfiltered grief that clung to the patients was a constant assault. The dim embers of hope in their eyes were a cruel counterpoint to the despair gnawing at his own soul.

A young girl, clutching a tattered teddy bear with one arm dangling limply by her side, stared at him with eyes that held the weight of the world. It was a look that pierced through his carefully constructed walls, a silent plea for a miracle in a place where miracles seemed truly impossible. The quiet desperation radiating from her tiny frame threatened to crack his composure, a stark reminder of the human lives already sacrificed in this brutal conflict.

The truth gnawed at Bruno. This wasn't a fortress; it was a collection of thin canvas sheets stretched taut against a hurricane. Every night, the drone strikes arrived with a mechanical wail, a tremor that shook the clinic walls and sent chills down his spine. Patients huddled together, their eyes wide and unblinking, reflecting the raw terror visible in Bruno's own reflection in the chipped mirror hanging askew.

Here, in the wreckage, the clinic clung to its existence like a fragile spiderweb. Doctors, their faces hollowed and eyes rimmed with exhaustion, fought a relentless battle against a tide of suffering that threatened to drown them all. Sleep was a stolen luxury, a brief respite between the constant moans of the wounded. The air hung heavy with the metallic tang of blood and the ever present threat of another bombing.

Yet, amidst the despair, the clinic remained a fragile ember of humanity. A weary counselor, her voice hoarse from countless conversations, offered a shred of hope, a desperate whisper that even in the darkest corners, the human spirit could still survive. But the light seemed to be dimming, its flame threatened by the relentless onslaught of war.

A stifling afternoon shattered by a whirlwind of dust and fear. Through the battered clinic doors burst a tiny figure, no older than eight, her storm-wracked eyes holding a terror that threatened her ability to breathe. Dr. Nadia, weariness apparent in her deeply lined face, knelt before the girl. A ghost of a smile, a fragile beacon in the suffocating darkness, coaxed the child onto the scarred examination table.

Bruno watched, a fist tightening in his gut like a vice. Nadia, with practiced hands that belied the battlefield they called a clinic, cleaned a jagged shrapnel wound on the girl's arm. Each touch filled with a tenderness at odds with the unrelenting cruelty that surrounded them.

Later, bathed in the dim, anemic glow of the generator, Bruno found Nadia huddled with the girl. The once pristine white walls were now a canvas of chaotic color—a desperate attempt at normalcy, a world built on the vibrant defiance of crayons. Nadia's voice, a rasp against the oppressive silence, weaved a tale that danced between fantastical creatures and the harsh reality lurking just beyond the clinic's flimsy walls.

As Bruno witnessed this stolen moment of peace amidst the wreckage, a glimmer of hope, as fragile as a butterfly with a broken wing, dared to ignite within him. This wasn't a war he could win with guns and tactics. Here, the enemy was despair itself, and the fight was for the embers of humanity glowing in the face of unimaginable loss.

The clinic wasn't a shield; it was a tenuous sanctuary, a bubble of embattled hope threatened by the ever present storm. Here, Bruno, the hardened emergency management coordinator, found a new purpose. He became the silent guardian, a bulwark against the encroaching darkness. He ensured the doctors and nurses could work without constant fear, that refugees could find a bit of solace in the storm's eye. His duty was to protect the fragile flame of hope, however tenuous, from being extinguished by the brutal realities that clawed at the clinic's walls.

Being experienced and calm wasn't about heroics or saving the day. Bruno learned the truth by serving in countless conflicts. Here, heroism was a luxury they couldn't afford. It was about keeping your head down, a steady rock in a churning sea of despair. You were a sandbag in a hurricane, yes, but not one that offered a temporary shield. You were the makeshift barrier constantly on the verge of collapse, offering a snippet of protection even as the storm raged on.

Bruno realized his skills weren't about grand gestures, displays of bravery quickly forgotten. It was about the quiet victories against the relentless tide of suffering. It was about using his experience to carve out a bit of normalcy in the heart of chaos, a fragile space where weary eyes could find a glimmer of hope, even if for a fleeting moment.

The faces that haunted Bruno's dreams weren't his own. They were the etched lines of worry on the mothers' faces, the vacant stares of children who had seen too much, the spark of life extinguished in those who didn't make it. This wasn't about him or his team. It was about those victims, the ones who had lost everything, clinging to the wreckage of their lives. Every life saved, every whimper soothed, was a tiny act of defiance against the despair that threatened to consume them all.

4

Echoes of the Unheard

Faces of Displacement

The unforgiving sun beat down on the corrugated tin roof of the makeshift hospital, turning the interior into a stifling furnace. The air thrummed with a low hum of human misery, a stark contrast to the chirping of a lone sparrow trapped in a vent. Bruno, his brow furrowed with worry, scanned the perimeter. The barbed wire fence, meant to deter intrusion, looked like a child's attempt at building a fortress against the backdrop of a world gone mad. Inside, every available space was crammed with humanity. Families huddled on thin blankets in hallways, defeated expressions drawn on their faces. Children, their eyes wide and vacant, played listlessly with the debris of their former lives. Every face was a story, documentation of the relentless violence that had ripped a community apart.

Aisha, the Weaver

In a corner, hunched over a makeshift frame, sat Aisha, the weaver. Her hands, gnarled with age, trembled as she held a half finished tapestry. Each wrinkle on her face seemed to tell a thousand stories, each thread woven a vibrant testament to a life richly lived. But now, the once vibrant colors lay muted under the harsh light. The bombs had stolen everything—her husband, her children, her grandchildren—a lifetime of love and memories reduced to a desolate heap of rubble.

A choked sob escaped her lips, a single tear tracing a path down a cheek lined with the deep sadness of a lost world. Her unfinished tapestry mocked her, a painful reminder of a life that would never be the same. Each stitch she had meticulously sewn held a memory—the joyous squall of a newborn cradled in her arms for the first time, the nervous laughter of her son's wedding as he fumbled with the rings, the shared laughter with her late husband beneath a starlit sky, their dreams whispered on the warm desert breeze. Now, the once joyful threads felt heavy in her hands, a burden that threatened to crush her spirit. Grief, a suffocating weight, pressed down on her chest, stealing her breath and blurring her vision. Yet, amidst the overwhelming despair, a flash of defiance sparked in Aisha's eyes. She wouldn't let the bombs steal her spirit, wouldn't let the violence extinguish the fire in her soul. With a ragged breath, she picked up a needle, its metal cool against her trembling fingers. Slowly, deliberately, she forced herself to take a single stitch, then another. It was a silent act of rebellion, confirmation of the enduring spirit of humanity that refused to be broken. The single tear continued its journey down her cheek, but this time, it wasn't just a tear of sorrow; it was a tear of hope, a promise whispered on the wind that even in the darkest of times, life finds a way to stitch itself back together, thread by fragile thread. Each stitch, a silent prayer, a whispered memory, a defiant act of creation in the face of destruction.

Darwish, the Teacher

A man shaped by the relentless hand of time, Darwish clung to memories that shone brighter than his present reality. At eighty years old, displacement was a familiar ache, a recurring nightmare that had haunted him since childhood. He carried the scars of his first flight from war, forced with his family to flee to Gaza. Seventy-six years later, his journey as a refugee continued—a man forever on the run, forever dodging the specter of death that seemed to stalk him relentlessly.

Darwish had grown up in the refugee camps, witnessing the quiet despair that gnawed at his family. He'd seen the resilience too, the determination to build a life even in the face of uncertainty. It fueled his own drive to learn, to become a teacher. Education, he believed, was the weapon against despair, the key to a brighter future for himself, his family, and his community.

Twice, the horror of war had snatched his children. In 2008, a strike obliterated his once grand family home, a cruel echo of the devastation unfolding around him now. When the current assault on Gaza began, they clung to the hope of staying put. But the relentless airstrikes shattered their fragile peace. A single attack reduced his wife, daughter, her husband, and several grandchildren to dust and memory.

Forced south to Rafah, a military checkpoint became another cruel twist of fate. Torn from the remaining shreds of his family, Darwish was allowed to pass with only two grandchildren, the rest—his children, his other grandchildren—vanished into the chaos. Imagine the storm raging within him—the suffocating grief for the lost, the gnawing worry for the missing, the desperate hope for any scrap of news, all layered on top of the responsibility to protect the two fragile lives clinging to him.

And yet, amidst the wreckage of his life, Darwish persisted. He could sometimes be heard humming old folk songs, his voice a fragile thread connecting him to a past where life held promise. He'd gather a small audience in the sterile hospital halls, weaving tales of his homeland, his voice laced with a quiet determination. He wouldn't fade into oblivion, wouldn't let his family's memory die. These stories, passed on like embers, were his defiance against loss, his flickering hope for a future where his family's land wouldn't be a forgotten dream.

For Bruno, Darwish became an unlikely source of solace. Witnessing the old man's quiet strength, his unwavering will to keep teaching, even in the face of such personal tragedy, was a balm to his own weary soul.

Jamal, the Fisherman

His weathered hands, once strong and sure from years of wrestling with nets and battling the sea, trembled as Jamal clutched the worn photograph. It was a talisman, a fragment of a life stolen. The picture showed a bustling harbor, a sea of colorful boats bobbing on the turquoise water. Jamal's own vessel, the *Sea Spirit*, sat proudly in the center, its name a cruel joke now. The harbor outside the clinic window was a graveyard. Splintered wood and twisted metal lay like the bones of fallen giants, a silent testament to the bomb's fury.

His gaze took in the desolate landscape. The vibrant blue of the ocean in the photo was replaced by a dull film of despair. Jamal didn't cry, not anymore. Tears had dried up days ago, replaced by a hollow ache that gnawed at his soul. The bombing hadn't just taken his boat, his livelihood; it had ripped away part of himself. His younger brother, Khalil, was gone. Their laughter, the rhythm of the waves against their boat, a lifetime of shared memories —vanished in a deafening roar and a flash of fire. They'd been at sea when the missiles rained down, their small craft a vulnerable target against the sky's fury. Jamal had returned to find only a smoldering wreckage and the news that shattered him.

Khalil wasn't just his brother; he was his fishing partner, his confidant, the one person who understood the unspoken language of the sea. Now, the vast ocean, once his playground, held only a chilling emptiness. The future stretched before him, an endless expanse as empty and desolate as the shattered harbor.

The burden on Jamal's shoulders had doubled. Not only did he have to support his own family, but now Khalil's wife and children relied on him too. In Gaza, where every drop of water and scrap of food is a fight for survival, the weight of responsibility threatened to crush him. Yet, even with his spirit fractured, Jamal wouldn't break.

Bruno saw the flare of defiance in Jamal's eyes, a silent refusal to surrender. He saw it in the way Jamal, despite his grief, chose to be helpful. He carried supplies, cleaned the floors, helped the wounded with a quiet stoicism. One day, Bruno, overwhelmed by the relentless suffering, confided in Jamal, "It feels impossible. How can anyone keep going?"

Jamal looked at him, his voice a rough rasp. "You don't have a choice, brother. You fall apart, and who suffers?

Your family, your neighbors, everyone around you. We keep going, not because it's easy, but because it's all we can do."

Jamal's words, raw and honest, struck Bruno hard. In that moment, Jamal wasn't just a man who had lost everything; he was a symbol of resilience, a witness to the unstoppable human spirit that refused to be extinguished, even in the face of unimaginable tragedy.

Yasmin, the Student

She clutched her textbooks, their worn covers the only tangible reminders of a life that felt like a distant dream. Just a few months ago, these very pages held the promise of a future brighter than the Gaza sun. She'd graduated top of her class, the culmination of years spent hunched over desks, fueled by late-night oil and an unyielding desire to heal. Her dream—to become a doctor, a hopeful promise so desperately in need—burned with a fierce intensity.

But the bombs had rained down like a malevolent storm, leaving nothing but dust and despair in their wake. Her school, once a vibrant hub of youthful energy, lay in ruins, a concrete carcass mocking the dreams it once nurtured. The education she'd toiled for, the future she'd meticulously planned, had vanished in a single, deafening explosion. The worst part wasn't the interruption to her studies, though the ache of unfulfilled ambition gnawed at her. It was the silence. The deafening silence where her family's laughter used to echo. Caught in the crossfire, they were gone. The image of their lifeless forms, burned into her memory, was a constant torment.

She had buried them all beside the rubble of their bombed home, the makeshift graves a heartbreaking sign of the cruelty of war. Her neighbors, those who clung to life in the ravaged city, had helped her. With trembling hands and tear-streaked faces, they had dug into the unforgiving earth, offering a final act of love and respect to the departed.

Tears, long held at bay, welled up in Yasmin's eyes, blurring the once familiar diagrams in her textbooks. Frustration, a venomous serpent coiling around her heart, wrestled with a yearning so profound it threatened to tear her apart. The injustice of it all, the future snatched away just as it was about to bloom, felt like a cruel betrayal. Here she was, clutching the tools of her dreams, rendered useless in this war-torn reality. A dry sob wracked her thin frame, her eyes squeezed shut in a desperate attempt to dam the flow of tears. But they wouldn't come. The well had run dry, leaving behind a raw ache that radiated through her entire being. In their place, a single, choked gasp escaped her lips, a silent scream for a life stolen.

Yasmin wasn't just a student anymore; she was a symbol of a generation robbed of its potential. Yet, amidst the wreckage of her world, a tiny ember of hope glowed. The textbooks, though battered, were still salvageable. The knowledge within them, a weapon against despair.

Bruno interacted with them all, offering a cup of tea to Jamal, a gentle smile to Yasmin, a moment of quiet solace for Aisha, checking on Darwish—these small gestures transcended language, offering a bridge of connection amidst the ruins. These were just a few stories from the much larger collection of suffering that unfolded within the clinic walls. Each day brought a new wave of displaced people, each face burdened with the trauma of war. There were the elderly, their bodies frail and their spirits broken; the young mothers, their eyes filled with a desperate fear for the safety of their children; and the children themselves, their innocence shattered by the violence that surrounded them.

One day, the clinic doors were flung open in a whirlwind of dust and fear. A child, barely five, stumbled in, his face streaked with grime and a raw, primal terror clinging to him like a shroud. Bruno's heart lurched—his injury wasn't a scraped knee or a feverish cough. This was a child sculpted by tragedy. His name was Karim, a whisper on cracked lips, the rest of his story etched in the haunted depths of his wide, vacant eyes.

Bruno recognized that look. It was a mirror reflecting a part of himself, a part buried deep from his own brushes with loss. He knelt before Karim, the floorboards groaning under his weight as if mimicking the burden pressing down on the boy's tiny shoulders. A granola bar, the only solace he could offer, felt pathetic in his hand. A tentative smile, practiced countless times on countless faces, stretched across his own.

Karim stared back, suspicion warring with a fragile, tentative hope flashing in his eyes. Bruno, his own throat tight with a grief he couldn't explain, pointed towards a corner of the clinic. There, a mockery of normalcy resided—a makeshift play area overflowing with donated toys, a desperate attempt to bring color to this monochrome world. With a gentle nudge, softer than a feather for fear of shattering the boy altogether, Bruno urged Karim to join the other children.

Their laughter, a melody both sweet and heartbreaking, sliced through the constant drone of warplanes overhead and bombs that erupted in terrifying bursts, momentarily cutting off their laughter and sending them scrambling for cover under chairs and tables. But then, with a resilience that defied their circumstances, they would pick themselves up, brush themselves off, and resume their play, the joy tinged with a newfound wariness. The bombs became a punctuation mark in their playtime, a grim reminder of the world outside the clinic walls. The sound of children's laughter didn't fit here, feeling like a betrayal of the horrors Karim had witnessed. But there, hesitant and clumsy, went Karim, drawn towards the light. A hesitant smile, a flicker on his lips, a single ray of sunshine managing to pierce the storm clouds in his eyes.

That evening, as Bruno meticulously reviewed security protocols with a weary staff, a lump formed in his throat as he stole a glance at Karim. The boy was now chasing a brightly colored ball with a giggle that echoed through the sterile room, a stark contrast to the devastation etched on his face just hours ago. It was a moment, a single, stolen breath of joy amidst the suffocating despair. A testament, however fragile, to the enduring spirit of childhood, a glimmer of hope refusing to be extinguished even in the darkest corners of a war-torn world.

The groan of the overloaded bus echoed through the dusty air, disgorging a tide of weary humanity onto the cracked pavement. People, their faces etched with the lines of a lifetime crammed into a single, horrifying week, disembarked. Amongst them was Sarah, a woman whose age wasn't a number but a story etched on her skin. Wrinkles, like canyons carved by a lifetime of hardship, fanned out from her tear-streaked cheeks. Each one held a memory—a war survived, a displacement endured.

Fleeing her home felt like a blur, a nightmare fueled by the relentless drone strikes that turned the night sky into a terrifying light show. The bombs themselves were a dull roar compared to the scream that tore from her throat as she was separated from her family in the chaos. Lost. Somewhere amongst the throngs of displaced people, her loved ones were gone.

Bruno watched, a leaden weight settling in his gut, as Sarah crumpled onto a rickety chair. Her body, already bowed by years, seemed to fold in on itself as wracking sobs erupted from her chest. Each one was a hammer blow to the fragile hope that burned within the clinic walls. A young volunteer, Marion, materialized beside her, a beacon of empathy in the sea of despair. Kneeling, Marion offered not just soothing words in broken Arabic, but the most precious gift of all—a silent hug. Sarah's tears, a torrent of grief and fear dammed for far too long, finally found release. They streamed down her weathered face, carving new lines alongside the stories already etched there. Marion, her own youthful eyes glistening with unshed tears, held Sarah close, a silent promise that amidst the wreckage, a shred of humanity still remained.

The days bled into weeks, each sunrise a cruel reminder of the relentless suffering that gnawed at the clinic's walls. Faces, marked by the narratives of war, became a haunting tapestry woven with the threads of suffering. Bodies, broken and lifeless, were carried in, a grim symphony of injuries echoing the constant bomb blasts. Funerals, hurried affairs conducted under a sky choked with smoke, became a daily ritual. Prayers, whispered pleas for solace and strength, mingled with the cries of the wounded and the whimpers of the dying. Even dreams, once a refuge, were now twisted by the ever present explosions, transforming into a battlefield where sleep offered no escape.

Bruno learned their stories, each one a shard of broken hope carefully collected. He heard of shattered dreams, of families torn apart, of homes reduced to rubble. He ached for them, a silent echo of their despair resonating within him. It wasn't just the physical wounds he witnessed; it was the soul crushing weight of unanswered questions. "Does the world even know what's happening to us?" they'd ask, their voices laced with a desperate plea for acknowledgment. "Do they not care? Does anyone out there even know we exist, and that we're dying?" Bruno, burdened by their plight and the helplessness of the situation, could only offer a comforting hand and a silent vow to be their voice, evidence of their resilience in the face of oblivion.

One evening, the call to prayer echoed like a lament across the ravaged landscape. Bruno stood on the clinic's rooftop, his gaze sweeping over the endless sea of tents that choked the horizon. The city was a shattered mosaic, a testament to the relentless cruelty of war. Yet, amidst the wreckage, life clung on with desperate defiance.

A group of children, their faces smudged with dust and hope, kicked a makeshift ball around a patch of barren earth. Their laughter, a fragile melody against the constant boom of explosions, was a poignant reminder. It reminded Bruno, Imane, Francois, and Marion, who had joined him on the rooftop, that even in the darkest corners, the embers of hope could burn stubbornly.

They stood there, united in a shared silence, each haunted by the faces that had passed through the clinic doors. Faces etched with the stories of resilience and unimaginable loss. Names like whispered prayers on their lips: Aisha with eyes that held the weight of the world; Jamal, the old man who clung to a faded photograph; Karim whose laughter had been silenced by loss, found joy and laughter again in the clinic, however fleeting.

The stench of death hung heavy in the air, a constant reminder of the human cost of this conflict. Broken bodies, with shattered dreams, lay amidst the rubble. The mournful wail of sirens and the relentless explosions formed a grim symphony of suffering. These were the resolute souls who had come seeking refuge, a sliver of hope in the storm, only to have it snatched away by the cruel hand of war.

A heavy silence descended upon them. Bruno felt the weight of their shared grief pressing down on him, a suffocating cloak. Hope, once a glowing flame, seemed extinguished, replaced by a profound sense of loss. Yet, as they looked at each other, a spark ignited in their eyes. A silent vow to carry on, to be the light of hope in this desolate landscape, for the memories of the fallen, and for the faint embers of hope that still dared to glow in the hearts of the children, their laughter a defiant melody against the backdrop of war.

5

The Fragile Sanctuary

When Walls Offer No Sanctuary

The relentless drone of an unseen aircraft vibrated through the air, a constant reminder of the city's vulnerability. Bruno peered from the hospital window, his gaze sweeping across the packed chaos of Rafah's streets. Hundreds upon hundreds of people—refugees, the lost searching for loved ones, the desperate seeking food for their families—all wandered aimlessly. He surveyed the maze-like streets, formerly vibrant pathways pulsing with activity, now reduced to lifeless concrete tombs. Skeletal remains of buildings cast long, ominous shadows that stretched across the ravaged landscape. Here, amidst the wreckage, Bruno faced a different kind of threat—a constant, oppressive force that hung heavy in the air.

THE UNPREDICTABLE LANDSCAPE

It was a living hell—a tormented existence where death and brutality reigned supreme. Airstrikes rained down with terrifying suddenness, leaving gaping craters in the earth—gruesome scars that pockmarked the landscape. Bruno knew Gaza was a tinderbox. Anywhere, anytime, could erupt into a scene of carnage. The supposed "safe zones" were a cruel joke. Danger lurked everywhere here.

Bruno spent his days hunched over his phone, meticulously scouring news feeds for updates on the ever shifting map of danger zones. But this map was a flimsy shield at best, a desperate attempt to impose order on the chaos. In reality, every street corner, every alleyway, held the potential for sudden death. Local residents, their faces etched with the weariness of constant fear, became Bruno's most valuable resource. Their whispered accounts—a child torn to shreds by shrapnel while playing in a park, a family vaporized in a market bombing—painted a harrowing picture of the city beyond the clinic walls.

Navigating this maze of potential human obliteration felt akin to a twisted game of chance without any defined rules. Every intake of breath in the fetid air shimmering with the metallic stench of devastation...every heartbeat heightened with panicked preparation for what could be the next burst of chaos erupting. It was the harsh reality of existence in the wasteland beyond any human control, where the unpredictable landscape delivered devastating blows ceaselessly.

THE FRAGILE INFRASTRUCTURE

Gaza's infrastructure lay in ruins, its hospitals mere shells clinging to the brink of collapse. Power outages, a relentless torment, plunged the facilities into an oppressive darkness. The siege choked off fuel supplies, and the once steady hum of electricity died with a final sputter. Fluorescent lights wavered in a death throe, then failed, leaving wards swallowed by an inky blackness. This darkness rendered vital equipment useless—incubators that once cradled premature infants in a cocoon of warmth and life support fell silent, their monitors flatlining in an unnerving quiet. Kidney dialysis machines, lifelines for patients whose own organs had failed, became inert hulks. Respirators, the rhythmic whoosh that had sustained countless lives through disease and injury, stood silent sentinels beside patients struggling for each shallow breath.

Frantic activity burned in the gloom. Doctors and nurses, their faces set with grim determination, moved with a desperate urgency. Headlamps strapped to their foreheads cast pools of light as they fumbled for battery-powered alternatives, a meager substitute for the sophisticated equipment now silent and useless without power. But even these backup systems were failing, their fading beams a stark reminder of dwindling reserves. Here, Nurse Imane, bathed in the faint glow of a mobile phone screen illuminating a medical manual, performed manual chest compressions on a young boy stretched out on a makeshift table. His shallow gasps echoed in the cavernous ward, a tragic reminder of their precarious situation. This scene, a desperate fight for life in the wavering shadows, was a descent into a medical dark age, a horrifying reminder of the true cost of the siege.

Water, once a constant, became a precious commodity. Bruno, a wartime water warden by necessity, implemented strict rationing measures. The once abundant flow from the taps sputtered to a cough, then died altogether. The precious reserves in storage tanks dwindled with each passing day, each drop a lifeblood for the sick and wounded. Basic sanitation became a luxury they could ill afford. The stench of overflowing toilets permeated the air, a breeding ground for disease that threatened to overwhelm their already stretched resources. Nurses, their faces grim with a mixture of disgust and despair, were reduced to using bottled water for the most critical hygiene tasks.

But bottled water was a finite resource as well. Deliveries that once replenished their stocks were now sporadic and unpredictable, further limiting the hospital's options. Rationing became a daily ritual, a constant negotiation between desperate need and the grim reality of their dwindling reserves. Bruno spent his nights hunched over spreadsheets, meticulously calculating how much water each ward would receive, how many precious drops each patient would be allocated. These were not abstract numbers on a page; they represented the difference between life and death for the sick and wounded entrusted to their care. The weight of that responsibility pressed down on him with each passing day.

Sewage systems, choked by the siege, overflowed, spilling fetid water onto the streets—a toxic moat encircling the hospitals. The very air they breathed became a potential health hazard for the already weakened immune systems of their patients.

Just beyond the hospital's walls, a scene of agonizing irony unfolded. A convoy of trucks, their once proud paint job dulled by the relentless desert sun and the passage of time, sat mired at the border crossing. The canvas tarps stretched taut over their beds seemed to sag under the weight of their life-saving cargo.

Their cargo, stacked on pallets beneath the relentless desert sun, was a lifeline—medical supplies that could mend shattered bodies, food to nourish the weak, and water, a most basic necessity, to quench the thirst of the sick and wounded. These vital provisions were tantalizingly close, yet utterly inaccessible, a cruel reminder of the bureaucratic labyrinth that choked the flow of aid. The border crossing, a chokepoint controlled by a distant authority, remained an impassable barrier. Days bled into weeks, weeks into months. The vital provisions moldered under the harsh desert sun, a constant torment for the doctors and nurses battling to save lives within the hospital's walls. With each passing minute, this bureaucratic paralysis exacted a deadly toll on the lives entrusted to Bruno's care. Each rasping breath, each pleading look from a patient, was a harrowing reminder of the cost of delay.

MANAGING **the Human Factor**

Bruno's burden extended far beyond the external threats. Within the clinic walls, he shouldered the immense responsibility of safeguarding a fragile peace among the staff. This diverse group was a microcosm of the conflict itself. Seasoned doctors, their faces etched with the stoicism of years spent in war zones, worked alongside wide-eyed volunteers, their youthful idealism battling a burgeoning fear. Cultural sensitivities simmered beneath the surface, language barriers creating frustrating misunderstandings. Yet, they were all bound by the invisible chains of a shared siege—a relentless pressure that threatened to crack their collective resolve.

The constant barrage of bombings formed a discordant backdrop to their work, an unrelenting rhythm that pounded against their already frayed nerves. Sleep deprivation, long hours under duress, and the ever present threat of violence gnawed at their resilience. The endless explosions, punctuated by anguished screams, sent tremors through the clinic's already weakened walls, a shocking reminder of their precarious existence.

Amidst the charred ruins, Bruno stood as the berated peacemaker, his pleas for restraint and unity drowned beneath recriminating screams as acrid as the smoke clinging to the splintered rubble. He moved amongst them, a solitary buoy battered by the tempests of anger and fear stoked white-hot by the merciless onslaught. The endless tide of savagery flooding through their doors eroded any dreams of solidarity.

Though Bruno's gruff voice rasped hoarse from bellowing over the din of hostility, he persevered as a mediator desperately trying to calm the roiling tempers. With furrowed brow, he implored the value of cohesion in the face of such catastrophic adversity. His calloused hands raised in appeals for reason amidst the swirling vortex of rage.

Dr. Nadia and Imane were indispensable allies in this Herculean effort. Their strength to deliver hope and compassion under the most extreme duress proved that unbreakable fortitude could flourish even amongst seemingly insurmountable despair.

As Bruno's throat strained raw from beseeching the masses, Dr. Nadia's soothing murmurs provided an anchoring balm to those unraveling at the seams. Her deft hands showing the path forward through this darkness. Imane became a spark fanned to an inferno of inspiration, her fierce determination rallying the most traumatized to cling to the embers of resilience.

This trio's tireless vigil to preserve the last vestiges of humanity stood as a defiant rebuke to the cyclonic forces threatening to extinguish all light. They embodied the truth that unity and perseverance could still triumph where hatred sought to reign. An unbroken bedrock upon which the most tenuous dreams of peace could endure the most savage of storms.

. . .

BUILDING ALLIANCES

For Bruno, the true peril did not lurk in the complex political landscape of Gaza, but in the omnipresent threat looming over the hospital's fragile sanctuary—the skies above. The local security officials posed no imminent danger; their tenuous agreements for neutrality offered a small mercy amidst the greater storm of violence engulfing the region.

In this cauldron of chaos, Bruno's greatest act of resilience was forging alliances and cooperating with the various powers holding sway over the area. While the indiscriminate airstrikes and artillery bombardments shook the ground and walls around them, he fostered a network of vital relationships that allowed the hospital staff to endure.

There could be no unilateral survival, no going it alone when the indiscriminate harbingers of death rained from the skies without warning or mercy. The deafening detonations tightened like a noose, offering grim reminders that their sanctuary existed as a mere fragile illusion temporarily spared by the storm's insatiable appetite for destruction.

Bruno recognized that no delicate political negotiations could halt the onslaught's inexorable advance on their own. But through deft diplomacy and the careful cultivation of strategic partnerships, he created an intelligence network that provided precious forewarning of impending strikes. Those vital offshoots of information helped them evacuate floors, reinforce defenses, and make life-or-death decisions on timing evacuations.

While distant thunderclaps brought momentary panic, he wondered *Is this the one that breaches our defenses?* Bruno's web of coalitions across fractious lines often responded with an answer before the dust settled. Each brokered alliance furnished another tendril in a watchtower of forewarning—allowing the staff to steel their resolve and make contingency plans rather than retreating blindly.

The situation remained untenably precarious, the bombardments seeming to grow inescapably closer with every passing hour. Yet Bruno's carefully nurtured web of partnerships became the hospital's lifeline—granting a degree of advance warning and agency that made perseverance possible in even the bleakest of conditions.

To build solidarity and trust amid such a storm of brutal violence was an act of stubborn defiance. But it was also a potent force multiplier, where the collective insights and shared intelligence strengthened the hospital's chances of both enduring and mitigating the worst of the omnipresent threats. Bruno's steadfast bridge building across partisan lines transformed the hospital from a helpless target into a hardened entity with a semblance of control over its own fate.

VIGILANCE AND PREPARATION

In the face of relentless bombing and the ever present threat of chaos, established procedures became obsolete relics. Here, amidst the choking dust and scattered debris of this war zone, they were forced to rewrite the rulebook on hospital security from scratch. Protocols were cobbled together on the fly, hastily scribbled on tattered scraps of paper and etched into the haggard faces of the dwindling staff. Bruno drilled them with insistent repetition on improvised evacuation procedures, his urgency a constant battle against their overwhelming exhaustion. Every drill, every practiced scenario, felt like a futile attempt to outrun an inescapable tidal wave of destruction.

Stockpiling essential supplies became an obsession

bordering on mania. Food, water, medical supplies—anything that might sustain them and the stream of wounded—was obsessively crammed into every available nook, crevice, and partitioned space. Sterile hallways morphed into makeshift pantries overflowing with haphazardly stacked crates of canned goods and bottled water. Administrative offices shed their former functions to become fortified emergency shelters, the walls plastered with hastily drawn maps and escape routes meticulously charted in the scattered moments between bombardments.

Bruno became a cartographer of despair, constantly redrawing the escape atlas as the frontlines shifted and battle raged through Rafah's streets. Each thunderous bombing, each plume of acrid smoke signaling a structure's obliteration, demanded a frantic revision to his diagrams—a desperate attempt to stay one step ahead of the ever-changing, constantly worsening reality pressing in around them from all sides.

Even within the hospital's tenuous sanctuary, safety was a fleeting concept practically alien in its scarcity. They painstakingly designated "safe zones"—A grim and painfully ironic term considering the unceasing news reports streaming in of hospitals bombed, sieged and transformed into hellish battlegrounds. These fortified corners and reinforced alcoves offered a mere sliver of hope, a desperate promise of temporary refuge amid the unrelenting storm of explosive fire raining from the skies.

Every minute, every hour, was a harsh lesson in improvisation and grit. A constant scramble to adapt guidelines and contingencies to the ever-shifting tides and remorseless ebb and flow of the war cascading through Rafah's streets.In this powder keg of a city, the ground rules of security, readiness, and survival were terrifyingly fluid—demanding a constant, formidable vigilance fortified by a perilously thin veneer of desperate hope. A faint, glowing hope that somehow, someway, they might persevere through the bombardments and chaos relatively unbroken, if not entirely intact.

THE TOLL **of Uncertainty**

The bodies, the tears, the agonizing screams—a grim orchestra of human suffering became the haunting, unavoidable soundtrack of their shattered lives. The incessant drone of surveillance aircraft buzzed ominously overhead, an unwelcome harbinger preceding the bone rattling thunder of explosive bombardments. This cacophony of war served as a horrifying conductor for the waking nightmare that had subsumed every aspect of their existence. The sights, the sounds, the acrid smells of smoke, ash, and burned flesh—this suffocating symphony of death and destruction seeped inescapably into their daily routines, threatening to drown out any fleeting memory of what normal life once resembled.

Yet perhaps the most insidious, unrelenting tormentor was the overwhelming uncertainty that gnawed at their tattered grip on sanity. Not knowing what fresh horrors the next distant wail of sirens or the ominous rumble of explosions silhouetted on the horizon might precipitate. The memory of the three drone strikes remained seared into their psyches—a permanent scar of trauma that would never fully heal.

Two of those strikes had rained cataclysmic destruction directly upon the hospital itself—the supposed sanctuary swiftly transformed into an apocalyptic vision of a battlefield. Hallways became choked with the broken bodies and blood of the dead and grievously wounded—civilians who had sought refuge from the violence, only to find themselves trapped in the crosshairs. The cold realities of modern warfare rendered the international laws and medical ethics they had devoted their careers to upholding as mere hollow formalities without any true deterrent against such barbarity.

The third strike targeted an unassuming residential building situated perilously close beside the hospital grounds. In a blinding, earth-shattering flash of white-hot oblivion, the structure and all its occupants were evaporated—the deafening shockwave rippling outwards like the primordial birth pang of a new circle of hell on Earth. Medics scrambled across the hospital grounds, pulling what tattered remains they could from the burning debris even as a deadly hail of shrapnel and shattered concrete continued raining down upon them and the terrified displaced families huddled in the courtyard desperate for shelter.

For Bruno, the world seemed to lacerate into visceral flashes of slow-motion clarity and kaleidoscopic distortion as the thunderous blast's concussive force slammed into him. He felt an excruciating pain erupt from his shoulder as shrapnel shredded through flesh—yet his consciousness seemed temporarily untethered from comprehending this reality. All he could perceive was the devastation unfolding in granular hyper focus before his disbelieving eyes. The anguished wails and panic of the wounded ringing with paranormal volume in his disassociated state.

Then, the primal instincts conditioned through years of trauma overrode his mind's self-protective fugue. Adrenaline flooding his system, he regained his footing and lurched back into frenzied motion—eyes frantically scanning for his medical team amidst the choking haze and apocalyptic landscape of rubble. A wave of relief crested over him as he saw their silhouettes emerging shakily—battered yet miraculously intact.

No words were exchanged in those first visceral moments, only a sustained wince of shared suffering and fatigue visible across their ashen, dust-caked faces. Medics instinctively triaged the myriad new injuries—adrenaline spiking heart rates masking the true depths of their own newly acquired wounds. Bloodcurdling screams pierced the ringing silence from the courtyard where displaced families had sought meager sanctuary—many now suffering grievous new lacerations from the shrapnel blizzard.

Bruno's gravelly voice issued a clipped volley of instructions, steady despite the unimaginable chaos unfolding. Medics rushed to triage the fresh casualties as others mobilized to evacuate the remaining civilians to the most fortified sections of the crumbling hospital's interior. It was a rehearsed pageant of pure desperation—life-saving protocols executed with practiced precision amidst the looming promise of total oblivion raining from the skies. A delicate ballet of compassion persisting defiantly in the face of unprecedented cruelty.

Yet, amidst the suffocating miasma of fear and grief that pervaded every crevice, a quiet but unbreakable strength continued. The medical team, the patients, the families trapped inside this waking nightmare—they clung to each other, forging an unshakable makeshift family united by the crucible of conflict. Small moments of shared camaraderie bloomed defiantly throughout the hospital's halls and wards—inside jokes passing between the evacuated refugee families, medics exchanging weighted glances and reassuring squeezes of hands as they rotated shifts, genuine sparks of human connection flaring to life amidst the omnipresent chaos raging outside the walls.

As the endless nights blurred one into the next, sleep itself became a cherished yet increasingly scarce commodity—its restorative embrace too often shattered by the jarring reality of their surroundings. Every distant boom and percussive shockwave reverberated through the very foundations, sending jolts of primal fear lancing through their already frayed nerves. Yet they persevered, pushing past the fatigue clawing at their eyes and lurching steps. Fueled by the newfound bonds of their tenuous brotherhood, an unwavering shared determination to shine as a sanctuary despite every attempt to destroy everything and everyone in its midst, pushed them ever onward through the bleakest hours.

These fragile human moments of respite, of supporting and caring for one another despite their disparate backgrounds and circumstances, became a united front against the relentless onslaught. Amidst unimaginable collective hardship and constant threats to their survival, they unexpectedly discovered untapped reserves of courage and perseverance—a powerful awakening to the enduring potential of the human spirit even under the most extreme duress.

Despite the ceaseless onslaught of challenges and setbacks, Bruno refused to surrender to despair. He harbored no idealistic illusions—even the most meticulously conceived contingencies and security protocols could be rendered asunder in an instant by a single well aimed missile or an unpredictable shift in the restless frontlines crisscrossing Rafah's shattered landscapes. Yet the option of acquiescing to fear's insidious spread was antithetical to his purpose.

The hospital stood as the last tenuous sanctuary in this urban war zone—its walls besieged by the thunderous bombardments shaking Rafah's shattered streets. Within, raw humanity clung to fleeting shelter with grim determination, a fragile glimmer refusing extinguishment amidst the apocalyptic devastation surrounding them. Bruno persevered alongside the few remaining staff, their wearied spirits soldiering on under immense burdens of responsibility. A dull, persistent ache weighed on everyone within the makeshift wards.

Yet whenever the encroaching shadows of despair threatened to eclipse their resolve entirely, flashes of defiant resilience blazed through the gloom. Makeshift beds overflowed with the torn and battered casualties of the merciless conflict, the sterile white walls intermittently bathed in flashes of crimson emergency lighting. Still, the faint cadences of clinging to life persisted—the ragged beeps of vital monitors, the labored yet shuddering inhales of the newly wounded arriving in waves.

In one corner, a young girl offered a fragile smile despite her obvious agony from her recently casted leg—a brave mask donned to soothe the worry etched into her parents' haggard faces. Elsewhere, a father clutched his injured son's hand in a death grip, eyes pleading wordlessly for any scrap of reassurance as Bruno made his rounds. It was these invincible human moments—the steadfast refusal to surrender basic dignity and hope for a semblance of normalcy—which breathed new fortitude into their ranks.

For the medical team, every agonizing hour of deprived rest, every near-miss as an airstrike's seismic fury shook the compound's very foundations, was rendered meaningful when met with such testaments to the enduring spirit. They would navigate the shifting labyrinths of peril. They would stanch bleeding wounds while striving to mend fractured souls ravaged by senseless cruelty. Above all, this stalwart vigil would be dutifully kept no matter how fiercely the tempests raged outside—for as long as the hospital's battered walls sheltered its fragile human souls within.

Here where life and death intersected in raw brutality, the rhythmic pulses of frayed humanity formed a defiant drumbeat celebrating the resilience of the unbeatable human spirit against annihilation. It echoed down the corridors, thrumming from sutured wounds and the tremulous blips of heart monitors—a solemn anthem venerating compassion's perseverance even when all order collapsed into apocalyptic ruin. The medical staff strove to uphold this sacred cadence, their collective resilience ensuring the fragile song of hope never fell silent.

6

A Haven Blooms

Acts of Compassion

The relentless drone of a distant aircraft grated against Bruno's frayed nerves. Inside the makeshift hospital, a discordant cacophony painted a heart-wrenching portrait of human suffering. The hiss of oxygen masks, the wet, hacking coughs of the wounded, and the choked sobs echoing through blood splattered corridors created a symphony of agony.

A palpable tension hung in the air—a suffocating blanket of hope and despair clinging to every soul within these battered walls. The fear of the next earth-shattering explosion loomed constantly, a morbid reminder of the chaos reigning just beyond the crumbling walls. It was a waking nightmare, the very air weighed down by collective anguish and terror.

In this grim tableau of suffering pushed to its breaking point, the line between hope and despair blurred. The hospital stood as a fragile bastion, a tenuous lifeline for those teetering on the precipice of oblivion. Yet amidst the unrelenting horror, an unspoken understanding persisted—a primal acknowledgment of their mortality and the unbreakable bonds forged in shared trauma.

It was this intangible connection, this raw determination to cling to the tattered shreds of humanity, which served as the only glimmer of light in the all-consuming shadow of war. For in the face of such adversity, the simple act of persevering became an act of rebellion against the forces seeking to extinguish the last embers of hope smoldering beneath the rubble of their shattered lives.

Bruno felt his heart fracture into jagged shards as he stepped into the pediatric ward, the cloying stench of fear and disinfectant enveloping him in a suffocating embrace. There, in the dimly lit corner, he spotted Layla, a fragile child who was just eight years old, huddled in the lap of Dr. Nadia. The once vibrant dress that had been an indication of Layla's lively spirit now hung in tattered remnants, clinging desperately to her frail, trembling form. Her eyes, once alight with innocent wonder, now held a haunting, hollow emptiness that spoke of an anguish no child should ever endure.

The world had borne witness to Layla's soul crushing agony, her tiny body buried beneath the merciless rubble, her anguished cries piercing the air as she pleaded for her loved ones. "Wait," she had begged, her voice raw with desperation, "don't save me yet. Find my Mama, Baba, please! My brothers, sisters!" It was a gut-wrenching example of the unimaginable cruelty of war, forcing a mere child to shoulder a burden that would break even the strongest of adults.

Layla, once a carefree spirit, had been thrust into the role of surrogate mother to her little brother Sami, a mere toddler of three, the sole survivor of the relentless airstrike that had obliterated their lives in a fiery instant. The deafening blast, the searing flash, the choking, acrid dust—these horrific, indelible memories were now etched into the depths of Layla's vacant, haunted gaze.

In the heartrending aftermath, Layla had emerged from the ruins to find Sami, his cherubic face streaked with grime and tears. Their parents, the pillars of their young lives, were gone, cruelly ripped away, leaving behind a gaping, bleeding wound that no number of bandages or soothing words could ever hope to heal. Layla's innocence, the very essence of her childhood, was forever swept away by the relentless currents of a war she could scarcely comprehend.

As Bruno watched the two siblings cling to each other, their small, battered bodies trembling with the weight of their shared trauma, he felt the overwhelming crush of their loss settle upon his own weary, burdened shoulders. In a world where the very concept of humanity seemed to have been abandoned, where the innocent lives of children were thoughtlessly sacrificed on the blood soaked altar of conflict, what hope could possibly remain?

Bruno's heart ached with a heaviness that threatened to steal his breath. Layla and Sami, mere wisps of children, sat huddled together, their eyes reflecting a depth of sorrow that no child should ever know. Their tiny bodies, dwarfed by the oversized t-shirts they wore, bore the telltale signs of a life upended—smudges of soot marking tear streaked cheeks, a vacant look that spoke of a stolen childhood. The weight of their unspoken stories, the invisible scars etched by violence, pressed down on him like a physical force.

Layla, her lower lip trembling, finally succumbed to the torrent of grief. Hot tears, silent and relentless, streamed down her soot stained face, each drop corroborating the unimaginable loss she had endured. Sami, sensing her sister's despair, burrowed deeper into Bruno's side, his small frame wracked with silent sobs. Bruno knelt beside them, the floorboards groaning under the weight of a shared sorrow. In that moment, a fierce protectiveness ignited within him. He wouldn't allow the storm raging outside to consume these fragile souls. He would be their shield, their fortress against a world that had failed them.

A silent vow echoed in the cavernous space of his heart. He would be the one to face the menacing drone strikes, the one to bear the crushing weight of their shattered reality. Within these walls, amidst the chaos and despair, he would fight to maintain this sanctuary. Here, they might find a bit of solace, a sliver of hope, however fragile, that would allow them to believe that even in the darkest hour, the embers of resilience could still glow.

Dr. Nadia had taken Layla under her wing. With a gentle touch and soothing words, she coaxed the girl from her state of shock. In the sterile confines of the ward, amidst the beeping of monitors and the hushed whispers of nurses, Layla found a semblance of solace. Dr. Nadia, with her infinite patience and boundless compassion, became the surrogate mother Layla desperately craved.

On that evening, as Bruno stood outside the ward, he witnessed Dr. Nadia reading Layla a storybook. The gentle cadence of her voice, the warmth in her eyes, created a pocket of tranquility amidst the chaos. Bruno saw a flash of life return to Layla's eyes. A tiny smile, a fleeting spark of curiosity, replaced the vacant stare that had haunted her since her arrival.

Seeing this interaction, a seed of hope, fragile yet tenacious, took root within Bruno. Layla, a ghost of a smile flickering on her soot stained cheeks, managed to build a tower of blocks with Sami, their giggles a melody defying the constant rumble of destruction. It was a small act, a fleeting moment of normalcy amidst the chaos, yet it bloomed like a single, defiant wildflower pushing through a crack in the war-torn concrete. In that shared laughter, Bruno glimpsed a flash of resilience, a tribute to the enduring human spirit that even the cruelest conflict could not extinguish.

Bruno's heart clenched as he witnessed another child, eyes wide with a confusion that unearthed his own buried memories, ushered through the hospital doors. The war had become a relentless thief, stealing not just lives and limbs, but the very essence of childhood. These children, some barely toddlers, others on the cusp of adolescence, bore the invisible scars of stolen innocence. Their families, shattered by violence, were scattered or lost altogether. The city stretched out beyond the hospital walls, a bombed-out wasteland mirroring the desolate landscape of their futures. Here, in this fragile sanctuary, they were adrift in a sea of uncertainty, each young face a haunting question mark. Who would care for them? Who would become their family in the wreckage of their world? The weight of their unspoken fear pressed down on Bruno, a suffocating cloak in the already oppressive atmosphere. He thought of an idea. *Perhaps, amidst the ruins, they could build something new, a haven where these fractured lives could begin to heal.*

Bruno found Dr. Omar in his office, a cramped space overflowing with medical charts and the ever present hum of worry. The director, a man once known for his jovial spirit, now bore the weight of the world on his shoulders. Yet, his eyes, though weary, still held a resolute spark, a hint of defiance against the storm raging outside.

"We need to do something for the children," Bruno began, his voice hoarse from the dust and despair that clung to the air. "Those who lost everything—their homes, their families..."

Dr. Omar nodded, a deep crease forming between his brows. "No one can look after them as everyone is overwhelmed and struggling to survive themselves. Even those with surviving family..." He trailed off, the unspoken reality hanging heavy in the air. Security and safety were luxuries few could afford in this war-torn city.

A fierce spark ignited in Bruno's eyes, a surge of determination piercing through the veil of despair that had settled over the hospital. "Then we'll be their family," he declared, his voice ringing with a newfound resolve that seemed to emanate from the very depths of his soul. Dr. Omar's worn, tired face broke into a weary smile, the lines etched by endless hours of strain and worry momentarily softening. It wasn't a perfect solution, not by any means, but it was a start—a glimmer of hope amidst the encroaching darkness that threatened to engulf them all.

Together, with the unwavering support of Nurse Imane, they hatched a plan—a desperate bid to create a sanctuary for the lost and broken children who had become the unwitting casualties of this relentless war. A wing of the already overcrowded hospital, previously used for noncritical cases, would be repurposed, transformed into a haven of solace and comfort.

Beds would be carefully pushed together, their metal frames scraping against the cold, unyielding floor, to create makeshift dormitories—a warm, secure place for the children to lay their heads after the horrors they had witnessed. A storage room, its shelves once laden with medical supplies and equipment, would be cleared out and lovingly converted into a playroom—a small oasis of innocence and joy amidst the chaos that reigned outside.

Doctors, nurses, and any other aid workers who were

willing to lend their time and energy would dedicate themselves to this cause, offering their presence and support to the children even after their own exhausting shifts had ended. It wouldn't be much—a roof over their heads, a warm meal to fill their bellies, a slice of normalcy in a world turned upside down. But most importantly, it would offer these vulnerable, traumatized children something far more precious: a sense of safety, a feeling of belonging, a semblance of the family they had so tragically lost.

Nurse Imane, with her gentle heart and unwavering dedication, would take on the responsibility of organizing the daily routines and schedules for this makeshift family. She would meticulously write down the needs of each child, ensuring that no detail was overlooked, no small comfort forgotten. Every bit of information, from their favorite toys to their dietary restrictions, would be carefully documented, a sign of the love and care that would be poured into this extraordinary endeavor.

In this small, cramped corner of the hospital, amidst the **overwhelming** chaos and suffering, a flicker of hope began to take root—a promise that even in the darkest of times, the unbreakable bonds of human compassion and resilience could light the way forward. For these children, who had seen far too much and endured far too much, this would be a chance to reclaim a piece of the childhood that had been so cruelly ripped away from them. And for Bruno, Dr. Omar, Imane, and all those who rallied around this cause, it would be a reminder of the invincible strength of the human spirit—a testament to the power of love and unity in the face of unimaginable adversity.

Bruno envisioned a haven within the storm. A place where children wouldn't just receive medical care, but where they could laugh again, cry without judgment, and feel the forgotten warmth of a hug. A place where they could start to heal, not just from physical wounds, but from the gaping hole ripped into their hearts. Maybe, just maybe, they could find a piece of the family they'd lost in the gentle touch of a caregiver, the shared laughter with a new "sibling," the simple act of being held safe and loved.

Bruno envisioned a sanctuary amidst the relentless chaos, a haven where children could find solace and comfort in the midst of unimaginable trauma. It would be a place where they wouldn't merely receive the necessary medical care for their physical wounds, but where their shattered spirits could begin the delicate process of healing. Here, in this oasis of compassion, they would be free to laugh again, their innocent giggles echoing through the halls like a defiant melody against the backdrop of war. They would be able to cry without fear of judgment, their tears met with gentle understanding and unwavering support.

In this haven, the children would rediscover the forgotten warmth of a loving embrace, the simple yet profound act of being held safe and cherished. It would be a place where they could start to mend, not just the visible scars that marred their bodies, but the gaping, invisible wounds that had been ripped into their tender hearts. Perhaps, within these walls, they could find a piece of the family they had so tragically lost—in the gentle touch of a dedicated caregiver, or the comforting presence of someone who understood their pain.

As news of the project spread like wildfire through the battered, war-torn city, it ignited a spark of hope in the hearts of those who had long been drowning in despair. Doctors and nurses, their faces etched with the indelible lines of exhaustion and sorrow, found a renewed sense of purpose in their weary eyes. Humanitarian aid workers, their own hearts heavy with the weight of the suffering they witnessed, stepped forward with unwavering determination, ready to lend their strength to this beacon of light amidst the darkness.

Even the grieving mothers, their own wounds still raw and bleeding, offered their hands to the children who had lost everything. They understood that it wasn't about replacing the irreplaceable—the loved ones who had been so cruelly snatched away—but rather about sharing what little solace and comfort they had left. In the act of reaching out, of offering their broken hearts to these shattered souls, they found a glimmer of healing for themselves as well.

With salvaged wood and discarded cloth, the volunteers and staff worked tirelessly to create play areas that would become more than just physical spaces. These rooms would echo not only with the laughter of children, but with the resilient spirit of hope that refused to be extinguished. Within these walls, stories would be woven, tales of courage and love that would forever be etched into the fabric of their young lives. Songs would be sung, melodies of comfort and joy that would chase away the nightmares that haunted their sleep. And through it all, a chorus of outstretched hands would reach out to the children who had been left adrift in a sea of grief and loss, guiding them back to the shores of hope and healing.

Affectionately dubbed the "Haven of Hope," the project began with a handful of frightened souls, children whose eyes had seen far too much, whose hearts had been shattered beyond recognition. But as word of their efforts spread, the story of this remarkable beacon of light in the darkness traveled far beyond the hospital walls. International aid organizations, touched by the depths of compassion and dedication displayed by Bruno and his team, sent volunteers and resources to support their noble cause.

Within a matter of days, the "Haven" had blossomed into a sanctuary for forty-seven orphans, proof of the unyielding power of the human spirit that could flourish even in the most desolate and war ravaged landscapes. This collective act of compassion transcended borders and ideologies, proving that even in the face of unimaginable hardship and suffering, hope could still take root and bloom.

In the midst of a world torn apart by conflict and cruelty, the "Haven of Hope" stood as a shining example of the unconquerable strength of love and unity. It was a powerful reminder that even in the darkest of times, when all seemed lost and the very foundations of humanity appeared to crumble, the unwavering commitment to compassion and kindness could light the way forward. For the children who had found shelter within its walls, the "Haven" represented not just a physical refuge, but a promise—a promise that they would never again have to face the storms of life alone, and that even in the face of unimaginable tragedy, they could still find a reason to hope, to dream, and to believe in a better tomorrow.

They started small, learning the rhythmic steps of the Dabke, a traditional Palestinian dance that had been passed down through generations. It was a defiant act of joy, a way for the children to reclaim a piece of their shattered culture and heritage. With each graceful movement, each synchronized step, they felt a glimmer of the pride and resilience that had been all but extinguished by the relentless violence surrounding them.

With salvaged crayons and scraps of paper, the children began to paint their dreams onto the stark, once bare walls of the Haven. Vibrant flowers bloomed from the depths of bomb craters, their petals a striking contrast to the gray rubble that littered the streets outside. Families held hands under a peaceful sky, their smiles an indication of the unbreakable bonds of love that persisted even in the face of unimaginable hardship. Slowly but surely, laughter, once a forgotten melody, began to fill the halls of the Haven, creating a symphony of hope that drowned out the distant echoes of war.

Among the children who found solace within the Haven's walls was Layla, a wisp of a girl who had arrived haunted by the weight of her own loss. Under the gentle care and guidance of Dr. Nadia and the dedicated volunteers, Layla began to bloom like a delicate flower pushing through the cracks of a war-torn landscape. A hesitant smile returned to her lips, gradually replaced by genuine giggles as she rediscovered the simple joys of childhood, chasing butterflies through the makeshift courtyard with a newfound sense of wonder.

As Layla started to draw again, her creations no longer depicted the scenes of destruction that had once plagued her nightmares. Instead, her colorful pages came to life with fantastical creatures and whimsical landscapes, a testament to the enduring power of a child's imagination to transcend even the darkest of realities. Watching her rediscover the pure, unadulterated joy of play, Bruno felt a lump form in his throat, overwhelmed by the significance of this small yet monumental victory. The war may have taken Layla's parents, but it could never steal the resilience that glimmered in her eyes, the unbeatable spirit that refused to be extinguished. Here, within the nurturing walls of the Haven, hope wasn't just an aspiration; it was a palpable force, a shield against the encroaching darkness that threatened to consume them all.

As the Haven of Hope flourished, it evolved into a

beacon of learning and growth, offering not only a safe haven but also a crucial lifeline of education to the orphans and children who had sought sanctuary within the battered hospital's walls. Among the displaced families who had found refuge in the building were teachers and social workers who had witnessed their own homes and schools reduced to rubble by the relentless bombardment. The devastating reality of the conflict was laid bare in the stark statistics: more than 200 educational facilities, including universities, had been targeted by airstrikes, with over 80 percent of Gaza's schools left severely damaged or entirely destroyed. The human cost was equally staggering, with 261 teachers and 5,479 students in Gaza bearing the brunt of the violence, their lives forever altered by the horrors of war.

With the conflict showing no signs of abating, an estimated 600,000 students found themselves cut off from their education, their futures hanging in the balance. Recognizing the vital importance of learning, even amidst the chaos and destruction, the dedicated educators within the Haven came together to create a makeshift curriculum, determined to provide some semblance of normalcy and hope to the children in their care. They tirelessly arranged lessons and courses, tailoring their approach to the diverse age groups represented, ensuring that each child had the opportunity to continue their education, no matter how dire the circumstances outside the hospital's walls.

As the fighting raged on, the Haven of Hope stood as a fragile oasis of peace and normalcy, its inhabitants acutely aware of the brutality that continued to plague the city beyond. The unrelenting frequency of bomb blasts cast long shadows even over this tiny sanctuary, a constant reminder of the precarious nature of their existence. Yet, within this small corner of the war-torn landscape, Bruno bore witness to a different kind of battle—a fight for humanity, compassion, and the future of children who had lost everything but their indomitable spirit.

In this fight, Bruno did not stand alone. Imane, a beacon of strength and devotion, played an integral role in the Haven's development. She embraced every child as if they were her own, pouring her heart and soul into creating a nurturing environment where they could feel loved, supported, and safe. Together with the doctors, nurses, and volunteers who had become a makeshift family forged in the crucible of war, they united in a common purpose: to build a sanctuary where hope could take root and flourish, no matter the storms that raged outside.

With resources stretched to the breaking point and the constant threat of bombardment looming over them, the guardians of the Haven of Hope drew strength from their unwavering belief in the power of compassion and their shared dream of a better future. They poured every ounce of their determination and resilience into creating a space where children could heal, laugh, and dare to dream again, even in the darkest of times.

Through their tireless efforts and unshakable dedication, Bruno and his fellow guardians nurtured the seeds of hope within each child, watching with a mixture of awe and humility as these fragile souls began to blossom. The laughter and dreams of the children became a defiant chorus against the backdrop of war, a manifestation of the enduring resilience of the human spirit in the face of unimaginable adversity.

In the Haven of Hope, a new chapter was being written—a story of love, strength, and the unbreakable bonds of a community that refused to let the flames of hope be extinguished. Though the path ahead was uncertain and the challenges seemed insurmountable at times,

Bruno and his companions drew courage from their unwavering commitment to the children who had become their family, their purpose, and their reason for believing in a better tomorrow. Together, they stood as a beacon of light amidst the darkness, a symbol of the unstoppable human spirit that could not be broken, even by the most devastating of circumstances.

7

Into the Mouth of Oblivion

Wrestling Hope from Gaza's Inferno

Bruno and his team had been closely monitoring the rapidly deteriorating situation in the northern part of Gaza, their hearts heavy with growing concern. The relentless bombardment had transformed the once thriving area into a hellish landscape, with countless civilians trapped amidst the rubble and chaos. Desperate pleas for help and harrowing reports of the dire conditions had been trickling in through various channels, painting an increasingly grim picture of the unfolding humanitarian crisis.

Orders from the Israeli military demanded the evacuation of hospitals in the north, forcing patients and staff to seek refuge in the southern part of the Gaza Strip. The injured and critically ill, unable to leave on their own, were left with no choice but to rely on the few ambulances permitted to assist in the evacuation. Those who could walk faced the daunting task of making their way south on foot, navigating the perilous, war-torn streets.

Faced with this heart-wrenching reality, Bruno and his team held urgent discussions, their voices laced with determination and trepidation. A daring plan took shape—a rescue and evacuation mission that would send them deep into the heart of the conflict zone. Their objective was clear: to save as many lives as possible from the besieged hospitals in the north and bring them to the relative safety of their own still functioning medical facility in the south.

Bruno met the gazes of his team, a well of steely determination mirroring the desperation in their eyes. It was a silent plea, a shared understanding that transcended words. With a deep breath, he accepted the familiar armor of responsibility. He couldn't shield them entirely, but he could lead them. Locking eyes with each member, a silent promise passed between them. They were in this together, a fragile band bringing hope as they ventured into the heart of a war zone.

AFTER MUCH DELIBERATION AND SOUL-SEARCHING, Bruno asked the team who wanted to accompany him on this perilous journey. A group of volunteers, their faces drawn with a mix of fear and unwavering resolve, stepped forward. These brave individuals, standing shoulder-to-shoulder with Bruno, were willing to put their lives on the line to save others.

The briefing was a grim symphony of whispers and tense silences, punctuated only by the scratch of pens on maps. The escape route, meticulously planned, felt like a cruel joke against the backdrop of the city's crumbling reality. Every member understood the inherent risk. They were a beacon in the storm—a tiny convoy of fluorescent vests and NGO logos, stark against the devastation. Every communication channel had been exhausted, every coordination confirmed. Beneath their stoic expressions, silent prayers flickered in their eyes. This wasn't just an evacuation; it was a desperate gamble, a fight for survival against all odds.

Those who remained behind, though their hearts ached to join the mission, understood the vital importance of their role in keeping the hospital running smoothly. They steeled themselves for the long, arduous hours ahead, preparing for the arrival of the evacuees and the challenges that would come with them.

As the ambulances pulled away from the hospital, the remaining team members watched with a potent mix of pride and heart-wrenching concern, their eyes glistening with unshed tears. Silent prayers for the safe return of their colleagues hung in the air, whispered from trembling lips. They braced themselves for the long, grueling hours that stretched before them, knowing that their work was just as crucial as those who ventured into the heart of the conflict. Together, united by an unbreakable bond of compassion and resilience, they stood as a beacon of hope and healing amidst the chaos, determined to bring light to the people of Gaza, no matter the cost.

The team lurched north, the once vibrant city before their eyes now unrecognizable. Streets choked with concrete rubble, flanked by buildings stripped bare to their skeletal frames. An oppressive silence reigned, broken only by the distant, guttural rumble of shelling. This wasn't just destruction; it was a graveyard, a city haunted by the ghosts of lives shattered in an instant. The weight of their mission hung heavy in the air, a reminder of the lives that hung in the balance and the horrors they were about to face.

. . .

Hope in the Rubble

THE WORD "APOCALYPTIC" felt like a stale understatement. This was a scene ripped from a dystopian nightmare made horrifyingly real. Rubble piled impossibly high, a testament to the massive scale of the devastation. Lives snuffed out, futures extinguished, memories buried under tons of concrete. How many bombs rained down to create this wasteland? The question hung heavy in the air, a silent scream with no answer.

As their convoy navigated the pre-determined route, the drone of unseen aircraft filled their ears. On the horizon, a fiery cloud erupted, smoke billowing skyward like a monstrous question mark. Then came the boom, a deep, shuddering concussion that rattled the very bones of the earth. The sound of war echoed around them, a relentless symphony of destruction.

The "hospital" loomed before them, a grotesque mockery of its intended purpose. The white flag, once a beacon of hope, now hung limp and tattered on a pole that leaned precariously to one side. The building itself resembled a shattered skull—gaping window cavities, once filled with life-giving light, now vacant like empty eye sockets. Black soot, like dried tears, streamed down the ravaged brick facade, evidence of the inferno that had raged here. The stench hit them first—a suffocating cocktail of smoke, decay, and something else, something metallic and acrid. They all choked back sobs that threatened to erupt, a physical manifestation of the despair in the scene before them. Every surface bore the scars of violence—jagged holes gouged by rockets, walls pockmarked by bullets. This wasn't just a damaged building; it was a battlefield hospital, battered and bruised, still stubbornly clinging to its role as a last refuge. The mission, already fraught with danger, felt like a desperate gamble in the face of such overwhelming devastation. Here, the fragile glimmer of hope they carried seemed swallowed whole by the gaping maw of despair.

Hours crawled by—each tick of the clock like a hammer blow against their already frayed nerves. Negotiations with the Israeli officers stationed outside the ruins were a high-wire act—a delicate balancing act between simmering frustration and the need for unwavering diplomacy. Bruno, a master of composure, kept his voice level and his expressions neutral, despite the fire that burned in his gut. He knew escalation could spell disaster, so he pushed down his anger and focused on the task at hand. Finally, after what felt like an eternity, a grudging nod of permission brought a burst of relief to his eyes.

They waded through a wasteland of debris, the air thick with a choking dust that seemed to carry the weight of unrealized hope. Inside the hospital, the scene echoed the devastation outside, only amplified. A cold dread settled over them as the distressing results of the violence unfolded—bloodstains smeared across the walls, the acrid tang of burned flesh clinging to the air. Here, amidst the wreckage, life clung on defiantly. Injured patients huddled in makeshift shelters, their faces gaunt and hollowed by despair. Haunted eyes, filled with a resignation that spoke of living deaths, watched their arrival with a hint of something akin to hope.

Bruno, ever the leader, stepped forward, the weight of responsibility a tangible presence on his shoulders. He knew any misstep could ignite a deadly confrontation. With practiced efficiency, he began coordinating the evacuation. Families, their faces etched with a mixture of fear and relief, were ushered towards the waiting ambulances and cars. His gaze fell upon a large area near the hospital door—a fresh, gaping wound in the earth. Cars, crushed like discarded toys, were piled high in a macabre mound by a bulldozer, a stark reminder of the brutality they had just entered.

The evacuation unfolded in a chaotic ballet of desperate haste and quiet empathy. The groans of the wounded filled the air as they loaded them into the ambulances, each silent promise of safety a balm on their own frayed nerves. But for some families, the bitter truth lingered. They were forced to leave loved ones behind, their bodies laid out like fallen heroes within the ravaged hospital. No time for goodbyes, no ceremony for the dead —the occupying forces held the hospital hostage, their cruel orders dictating every move.

Hours morphed into an eternity as they waited for passage back south. The tension in the convoy was a living thing, a suffocating weight that pressed down on their chests. Every rumble in the distance, every flicker of light on the horizon, sent tremors through the team. Bruno and his crew exchanged worried glances, a silent language of shared fear and frustration. Words seemed like hollow echoes in the face of such immense uncertainty. The air crackled not just with dust, but with the raw electricity of their collective apprehension. They were trapped in a game where the rules changed on a whim, and the stakes couldn't be higher.

Finally, the green light. Relief washed over Bruno, a wave that threatened to drown the knot of tension that had tightened in his gut for hours. But as they pulled out, the devastation that surrounded them offered a stark reminder of their precarious situation. They were driving south, a caravan of hope amidst the ghosts of a city. Buildings, roads, everything—pulverized into unrecognizable rubble, a devastating sign of the war's insatiable hunger.

They raced south, a fragile bubble of life hurtling through a nightmare landscape. Every turn, every rise in the road, held the potential for another ambush, another near-miss. The pounding of the engines echoed the incessant rhythm of the bombing in the distance, a grim reminder of the fragility of their existence. With each mile they covered, the weight on Bruno's chest did lessen, but it wasn't replaced by pure relief. It was a glimpse of hope, a desperate prayer whispered against the ever present roar of war, a plea that they wouldn't become another casualty in this senseless conflict. The journey south was a tightrope walk between hope and despair, a race against time and the ever present threat of oblivion.

Back at the southern hospital, a semblance of order battled against the tide of chaos. Medics, faces marked with exhaustion and grim determination, rushed to unload the patients. Each gurney was a fragile boat carrying a life across the turbulent sea of war. Inside, within the relative safety of the wards, they fought a new battle—a desperate struggle to heal wounds with the meager resources at their disposal.

Meanwhile, families spilled out of the ambulances, lost souls adrift in a storm of confusion. Some stumbled blindly, searching for a familiar face amidst the sea of displaced humanity. Others huddled together, whispers like withered leaves swirling around their grief. The air throbbed with the raw sounds of despair—cries erupting from throats choked with loss, the wail of a mother searching for a child who might never return.

And then, there were the missing. Unnamed ghosts haunting the periphery of existence. Underneath tons of rubble, some lay silent and unknown, their stories buried with their bodies. Others, scattered amongst refugee camps, played a cruel game of chance—every day a gamble between life and death, freedom and abduction.

Hope in the Rubble

The Israeli prisons, silent leviathans on the horizon, swallowed some whole, their fates a chilling mystery.

Silence, thick and heavy, descended upon the remaining members of the convoy. It wasn't the restful silence of relief, but the solemn acknowledgement of a shared trauma. That night, sleep wouldn't come. Behind closed eyelids, a merciless slideshow of horror flashed: bodies contorted in agony on shattered streets, buildings reduced to skeletal husks, and the hollow, haunted eyes that spoke of unspeakable suffering. An overwhelming urge to scream, to document the barbarity, seized Bruno. He poured over photographs and videos taken during the evacuation, each image a stark reminder of the human cost of war. In their stark brutality, they served as a necessary jolt—a desperate measure to combat the numbing silence that threatened to swallow him whole.

Later that night, Bruno initiated a FaceTime call with Ronnie back in Scotland. Ronnie wasn't just a colleague; he was the anchor in Bruno's storm, the one who understood the invisible burdens he carried. Ronnie was their walking encyclopedia, the answer to any work-related question. But tonight, Bruno wasn't calling for facts or figures. He needed a lifeline, a connection to a world untouched by the horrors he'd witnessed that day.

As Bruno recounted the events in broken fragments to Ronnie's pixelated face on the screen, a flicker of his old self flashed across the screen. A faint smile tugged at the corner of Bruno's lips, coaxed out by Ronnie's characteristic sense of humor coming through the phone's speakers. A dark chuckle rumbled between them. "Well," Ronnie quipped, "at least this time you brought back more people than you left with!"

It was a weak attempt at humor, and Bruno winced, the weight of the joke settling heavily on him despite how much he'd enjoyed the lighthearted tone of the video call until now. Ronnie instantly sensed the shift in mood through the camera. "Seriously though," he amended hastily, "good work getting everyone back in one piece. We can't all be heroes, but at least we're not target practice, right?"

The reference was a gut punch. A shared memory of a close call in a past mission, a moment they'd faced with gallows humor and a shared hope that had gotten them through. In that shared memory, Bruno found a bit of solace. Ronnie wasn't offering solutions or trying to erase the trauma. He was simply acknowledging it, offering a familiar voice in the darkness, a reminder that Bruno wasn't alone in carrying the weight of this war. The call ended with a shared sigh, a silent understanding hanging heavy in the air between them. But for a brief moment, the camaraderie had pushed back the darkness, proof of the enduring power of human connection even in the face of unimaginable hardship.

8

Choices and Sacrifices

Hunger, Thirst, and the Fight for Survival

The weight of a thousand decisions pressed down on Bruno like an unyielding stone. Each sunrise brought a fresh dilemma, a new fork in the road marked only by question marks. Every choice felt like a gamble, not just for his own well-being but for the staff and patients who clung to the hospital as their last vestige of hope.

Hunger gnawed at his insides, a constant companion in the daily struggle to secure basic necessities. The hospital, once a beacon of healing, now resembled a glowing candle, threatened to be snuffed out by the siege that strangled the city. Over a million refugees crammed into their fractured city, each face a silent plea for a miracle.

Bruno watched snippets of news reports on a borrowed phone—grainy images of protests and demonstrations erupting around the world, a chorus of voices demanding a ceasefire. Musicians released songs, artists created murals, all pleading for an end to the bloodshed. Here, however, blood flowed freely, a grim currency demanded by the unseen forces controlling their fate. Did it take broadcast images and videos of bloodshed for the world to see their suffering? Even with the global outcry, the bombs continued to fall, a cruel symphony of destruction. Despair threatened to engulf him, but Bruno clung to the faces of the staff, their unwavering dedication a flickering ember against the encroaching darkness. He couldn't afford to give in. He was their leader, their anchor in this storm, and even if the world seemed deaf to their plight, Bruno wouldn't let them be forgotten.

Dr. Nadia came to see Bruno, her eyes burning with a desperate plea that resonated in his gut. Bruno, a master of reading body language, understood the unspoken urgency in her posture, the tremor in her voice that went beyond the words themselves. "Medical supplies," she rasped, "we're down to a two-day trickle. We need the central depot. They might have gotten a new shipment."

Bruno's heart sank. The central depot, once a lifeline, had been bombed during the war. The attack, which claimed the lives of UN staff, was a stark reminder of the dangers beyond the hospital walls. Now, though it was patched up and operational again, it felt like a gamble just to get there. The route itself was a war zone—bombed-out buildings, sniper alleys—every trip outside was a morbid dance with death disguised as a desperate bid for survival. He clenched his fists, the weight of the decision pressing down on him. The risk was high, but the alternative was unthinkable.

To stay put was to watch their meager supplies dwindle, to witness patients succumb to treatable illnesses. The image of the young boy with the festering shrapnel wound flashed across his mind, followed by the frail woman struggling with pneumonia. Their hopeful eyes, their fragile trust—he couldn't let them down.

Hope in the Rubble

Bruno, the gravity of the situation heavy on his shoulders, huddled with Dr. Nadia and the senior staff. Together, they meticulously planned the route to the central depot, factoring in known sniper nests and potential risks. They assembled a team, their faces grim masks of fear and determination. With limited communication, they desperately contacted anyone who might grant them passage to the depot. But their pleas were met with a wall of resistance. The risks were too high, the potential for casualties too great. The green light they craved never appeared.

Refusal only hardened Bruno's resolve. He meticulously planned the route, dodging known sniper nests and navigating the gauntlet of bombed-out buildings. He rallied the staff, their eyes reflecting the same mix of fear and determination he felt. They pooled their meager resources, packing rations into backpacks alongside essential medical supplies. The air hummed with nervous energy as they loaded the rickety ambulance, a vessel carrying not just medicine, but the fragile hope of a beleaguered hospital. The drone of unseen aircraft filled the tense silence, punctuated only by the ever present rumble of distant bombs, a grim reminder of the war that raged all around them.

The journey was a grueling test of nerves and resilience. Their clearly marked NGO ambulances and cars were a token of protection in a war zone, a desperate hope that drone pilots would respect international law. Each rumble in the distance sent shivers down their spines, a potential death knell disguised as thunder. They navigated a labyrinth of shattered concrete and twisted metal, the stench of decay clinging to the air like a shroud. Buildings, once vibrant testaments to life, now stood as hollow husks, silent witnesses to the city's suffering. Yet, Bruno and his team pressed on, fueled by a shared purpose that transcended fear. It was a silent oath whispered not in words, but in the determined set of their jaws and the unwavering glint in their eyes.

They reached the depot, a scene of controlled chaos. Supplies were a trickle compared to the desperate need, and shortages were evident on every face. The distribution process felt agonizingly slow, each tick of the clock a hammer blow against their dwindling patience. Frustration simmered, a tangible presence in the air, but they refused to give in. Finally, after an eternity of waiting, they emerged with a fresh stock of bandages, antibiotics, and painkillers—a meager haul, yet a lifeline for the hospital they held dear.

The return trip was just as perilous, but a sense of accomplishment buoyed their spirits. Back at the hospital, Dr. Nadia's face broke into a relieved smile as they unloaded the precious cargo. The weight lifted from Bruno's chest was palpable, replaced by a fleeting sense of victory.

But this victory was short-lived. The siege remained, a suffocating python squeezing the life out of the city. Water, once abundant, became a precious commodity, rationed with a miser's hand. The overflowing wards served as a grim tide, further evidence of the war. Human bodies spilled out of rooms designed for sterile efficiency, each one a story of suffering etched in flesh and bone. Doctors and nurses, some bearing the invisible scars of personal loss, toiled tirelessly. Raw determination fueled their actions as they fought to save lives with whatever meager resources remained. Bruno saw the unshed tears glistening in their eyes—grief, a constant companion they pushed down for the sake of their patients. There was no time for mourning, no space for sorrow. The war remained an ever-present threat, a symphony of bombs and death, a grim reminder of the brutal reality that surrounded them.

The hospital, once a gleaming beacon of healing, now resembled a defiled cathedral. Its sterile walls, once pristine, were stained with the grime of war. Basic equipment, once the heart of modern medicine, lay broken on the floor, replaced by desperate inventions cobbled together with hope and duct tape. Electricity flickered like a dying heartbeat, plunging the wards into an oppressive darkness punctuated only by the occasional flicker of a lighter. Yet, even in this tomb of shattered dreams, a spark of humanity refused to be extinguished. Refugees, driven from their homes, found refuge within these crumbling walls. Huddled together, they shared their dwindling rations, cooking meager meals over makeshift fires beneath gaping holes in the roof. Stories of shattered lives were whispered in the glimmering light, a haunting chorus of loss and displacement. Children, whose eyes had already witnessed enough suffering and loss for several lifetimes, tried to recapture a bit of their lost innocence through impromptu games. Their laughter, a fragile melody against the relentless drone of destruction outside, was a defiant example of the human spirit's will to survive, even in the face of an unimaginable tragedy.

Bruno stood in the heart of the makeshift world within the hospital walls. It was a human tapestry woven with threads of despair and resilience. Funerals, hushed and hasty, punctuated the air with a heavy finality. Cries of the wounded echoed alongside the choked sobs of those who mourned. Yet, amidst the suffering, seeds of defiance remained. A child's smile, bright and fragile, bloomed like a rare flower pushing through cracked pavement. A shared laugh, born of gallows humor, rang out, a fleeting challenge to the ever present darkness.

A specter far more terrifying than any bomb loomed over Bruno and his team: a critical depletion of medical supplies. Once-functional hospitals, now better described as war ravaged shells, stood as grim documentation of the crumbling healthcare infrastructure. The influx of patients with penetrating injuries from explosions (polytrauma) and blast injuries (barotrauma) overwhelmed the limited surgical capacity. Even for those fortunate enough to avoid such trauma, the situation was dire. Chronic conditions became a terrifying death sentence for many, as essential medications like chemotherapeutic agents dwindled, leaving cancer patients without hope. Diabetics faced a similar fate, their bodies rebelling without access to insulin, a vital hormone regulating blood sugar levels. The already precarious situation for patients with chronic kidney disease (CKD) spiraled further as dialysis machines became inoperable due to power outages or lack of replacement parts, leaving them with a toxic buildup of waste products in their blood.

Beyond the immediate casualties, the unsanitary conditions in displacement camps created a breeding ground for infectious diseases. Outbreaks of waterborne illnesses like diarrhea (gastroenteritis) and hepatitis A became commonplace, straining the already depleted stocks of antibiotics and rehydration fluids. Respiratory illnesses, including pneumonia and tuberculosis, also took hold, fueled by overcrowding and inadequate ventilation. The psychological toll was no less devastating. The constant threat of violence, the loss of loved ones, and the displacement from homes all contributed to a surge in cases of post-traumatic stress disorder (PTSD), anxiety, and depression. Mental health services, already stretched thin before the conflict, were now woefully inadequate to address this burgeoning crisis.

Hope in the Rubble

Each day was a gut-wrenching exercise in triage, forcing Bruno and his team to make torturous decisions about who could be saved with the limited resources at their disposal. The crushing weight of this responsibility, coupled with the knowledge that countless lives were lost due to a lack of basic medical supplies, was a constant reminder of the barbaric nature of war and its devastating impact on even the most fundamental right: access to healthcare. Bruno and his team became not just medical providers, but also beacons of hope in a world shrouded in despair. They were a beacon of light in the face of unimaginable darkness.

Beyond the crushing weight of medical shortages, a specter of a different kind loomed large: malnutrition. The siege strangled the flow of essential foodstuffs, creating a devastating impact on Gaza's population. Basic dietary needs, the very foundation of human health, were left unmet. Children, particularly vulnerable due to their high metabolic demands, suffered from stunting and wasting, their bodies robbed of the essential building blocks for growth and development. This micronutrient deficiency manifested in a myriad of ways, from weakened immune systems leaving them susceptible to opportunistic infections (like nosocomial infections acquired in the hospital) to impaired cognitive development. Even for pregnant women and new mothers, a time of heightened nutritional needs, access to adequate food was a distant dream. This resulted in a rise in maternal anemia, a condition characterized by a deficiency in red blood cells, leading to complications during childbirth and hindering their ability to properly care for their newborns. Neonatal mortality rates soared as newborns lacked the crucial colostrum, the first milk produced by the mother, rich in antibodies and essential nutrients for a healthy start in life.

The situation within the hospital walls mirrored the despair outside. Bruno, witnessing the plight of his team—doctors and nurses battling exhaustion yet constantly gnawed by hunger—knew he had to act. The sight of displaced families within the hospital, their gaunt faces etched with worry as they struggled to secure even the most basic rations for themselves and their loved ones, particularly the orphaned children, was a constant source of heartbreak. Driven by this desperate need, Bruno embarked on a relentless pursuit of securing additional food supplies. He meticulously planned logistics, navigating a perilous landscape to source essential foodstuffs like fortified milk powders for children, prenatal vitamins for pregnant women, and iron supplements to combat anemia. While these efforts were a drop in the ocean compared to the immense need, they provided a glimmer of hope, a temporary reprieve from the gnawing hunger that threatened to consume them all. The Haven of Hope, with its ever-growing number of children, presented a similar challenge. Bruno tirelessly worked to ensure a steady flow of provisions, a constant battle against dwindling resources and the ever present danger of violence that hampered transportation and movement within supply chains.

The televised spectacle of humanitarian airdrops over Gaza offered a glimmer of hope, a fleeting respite from the crushing weight of shortages. However, seasoned aid workers like Bruno were acutely aware of the limitations and inherent dangers associated with this method of delivery. While airdrops provided a rapid influx of supplies, the quantities paled in comparison to the immense needs of the population. A single truckload, meticulously planned and delivered through established ground routes, could carry four times the amount of humanitarian aid compared to a bulky aircraft. Furthermore, ensuring equitable distribution of airdropped supplies proved a logistical nightmare. Vulnerable populations, including women, children, the elderly, and the infirm, were often physically unable to reach scattered drop sites, further exacerbating existing inequalities.

Tragically, the desperate scramble for airdropped supplies turned deadly on numerous occasions. Several documented incidents involved civilians being crushed by falling crates or drowning in attempts to retrieve packages from the sea. The unpredictable nature of airdrops often resulted in deliveries landing in active conflict zones or inaccessible border areas, further hindering their effectiveness. Despite the inherent risks, Bruno, along with countless others, witnessed the heart-wrenching sight of civilians putting their lives on the line, driven by the primal urge to secure even the most meager provisions for their families.

Water, a vital resource integral to survival and public health, is critically scarce in Gaza. The ongoing siege has severely restricted access to potable water sources, while airstrikes have compounded the crisis by systematically targeting and destroying essential water infrastructure, including wells and water tanks. This has left over 2 million residents grappling with severe water shortages.

According to the World Health Organization (WHO), the recommended daily water usage per person for basic needs is approximately 5.3 gallons (20 liters). For more comprehensive needs, the recommendation increases to around 26 gallons (100 liters) per person per day. However, since the onset of the conflict, the average daily water consumption in Gaza has precipitously declined to a mere 3/4 of a gallon per person. Most of which is contaminated. This stark reduction is insufficient for basic hygiene practices and essential daily activities such as sanitation, personal hygiene, and food preparation. A minimum intake of one gallon per day is necessary to prevent dehydration and its severe health consequences, including organ failure and systemic damage.

Currently, water trucking remains the primary distribution method, but logistical challenges such as damaged roadways and a critical shortage of fuel have rendered this method increasingly untenable.

Bruno's tenacity in liaising with the NGO proved fruitful. He secured their buy-in regarding the critical water scarcity issue at the hospital. Through effective advocacy, he fostered a collaborative partnership to implement a robust, stand-alone water purification system. This system leverages photovoltaic panels for electricity generation and incorporates battery storage to guarantee uninterrupted operation during grid outages. This vital equipment constitutes a significant improvement in the hospital's capacity to deliver potable water to both patients and staff. While the solution has limitations in scale, it represents a crucial intervention that fosters optimism within the community.

Bruno watched the water system installation, his heart a lead weight in his chest. He analyzed, assessed, strategized—but a deeper battle raged within him. Each life he touched, each story he heard, carved a deeper line into his soul. He yearned for the war to end, for the laughter to ring out without the echo of bombs, for the smiles to be untainted by the shadow of fear. But the weight of reality pressed down on him—the impact of this war would be etched forever on these walls, in these lives, and in his own weary heart.

9

Endings and Beginnings

A Farewell to Rafah

A heavy tension choked the air, a suffocating cloak woven from sorrow and despair. Bruno's mission in Rafah, a whirlwind of desperation and fleeting hope, was drawing to a close. The battered cars, their once proud emblems faded by dust and hardship, stood ready to whisk the team away from the city's ravaged heart.

The goodbyes were heart-wrenching. Bruno and his team had become more than just aid workers to the people they served; they were a lifeline, a hint of hope amidst the devastation. The act of handing over the reins to the new delegate felt like leaving a child in a burning house—an overwhelming responsibility that gnawed at them. These weren't just colleagues they were briefing; they were entrusting them with the weight of untold stories, The echoes of whispered prayers for peace mingled with the thunderous explosions of bombs.

There were no simple instructions to leave behind. Bruno could meticulously map out the established network, detail the logistical intricacies, and even sketch a grim blueprint of the ravaged landscape. But how could he possibly convey the bone-deep exhaustion that clung to every resident, the hollowness in the eyes of children who no longer dared to dream? The war, a monstrous entity, had left its mark on every soul, twisting lives and shattering innocence.

The biggest hurdle loomed large—the very systems and procedures that formed the backbone of humanitarian work felt flimsy here, mere cobwebs against a relentless storm. Safety was a fleeting illusion, and the effectiveness of their efforts remained a constant question mark. Yet, Bruno knew he couldn't succumb to despair. He had to instill in the incoming team the unwavering spirit they'd all cultivated—a spirit forged in the crucible of suffering. It was a spirit that demanded action, fueled by hope, a spirit that refused to compromise on the quality of their work despite the unforgiving reality that surrounded them. He had to empower them to navigate the treacherous path ahead, to be the steady hand that held onto the fragile threads of humanity in the face of unimaginable chaos.

But the war, a monstrous beast with an insatiable hunger, showed no signs of relenting. Its grip seemed to tighten with each passing hour, squeezing the lifeblood out of Rafah. The streets, once vibrant arteries of commerce and life, lay silent and deserted, their surfaces scarred by the brutal choreography of bombings. Buildings, like hollowed-out bodies once teeming with activity, gaped skyward like silent screams. Schools, universities, hospitals —the pillars of a functioning society—lay in ruins, stark evidence of the savagery that had unfolded here. Bruno felt a wave of nausea rise in his throat, a physical manifestation of the despair that clung to this ravaged city. He was leaving, but Rafah, and the ghosts of what it once was, would forever be etched on his soul.

Hope in the Rubble

The siege wrapped its suffocating coils around Rafah, an unyielding vise squeezing the life out of the city's hope. Daily pronouncements threatened a full-scale occupation, a horrifying prospect considering the city had already endured relentless strikes. The world used words like "incursions" and "skirmishes," failing to capture the true brutality that unfolded on Rafah's streets. The people there, their eyes reflecting every kind of loss imaginable, braced themselves for an unknown future.

Yet, amidst the despair, flickered a defiant flame. Doctors, nurses, and ordinary citizens who refused to abandon their homes became living testaments to an extraordinary resilience. Their weathered faces, etched with hardship but resolute, were a silent rebuke to the world's indifference. These were not just faceless victims in news reports; they were doctors fighting a losing battle against a tide of injuries, nurses offering comfort amidst the chaos, and families clinging to a shred of normalcy in a shattered world. Pawns in a larger game, perhaps, but pawns who refused to be played without a fight. Their courage, a quiet roar in the face of deafening silence, despite the apathy and lack of support they felt from the rest of the world.

Bruno stood amidst the throng of refugees, a sea of faces forming a heartbreaking mosaic of fear and defiance. Each story, carved into the lines chiseled on their weary brows and tearstained cheeks, echoed the grief gnawing at his own heart. This departure was different. In past missions, a bit of relief usually accompanied the escape from a war zone. But here, amidst these unlikely allies who had become a makeshift family, a part of him yearned to stay.

The weight of their shared struggles pressed down on him. He had witnessed their resilience, their quiet heroism in the face of unimaginable hardship. He saw in their eyes the same determination to survive that burned within him. Leaving felt like abandoning a post, turning his back on the fight they were waging not just for their lives, but for their very existence. The pull to stay, to stand shoulder-to-shoulder with them, warred with the responsibility of his own mission and the promise of a world untouched by the conflict. It was a brutal choice, and Bruno felt the weight of it settling heavily on his already burdened shoulders.

Bruno's steps echoed as he crossed back over the border, each one a thud against the hollowness that had taken root within him. Leaving Rafah felt like tearing a piece of his soul from his body. He yearned for the normalcy of home, for the simple comfort of a life untouched by war. Yet, the images that haunted him were an unrelenting barrage—the tear-streaked faces of children, the vacant eyes of the dying, the quiet desperation marked on every brow

How could he laugh again, knowing their laughter had been silenced? How could he savor a meal when their bellies ached with hunger? How could he quench his thirst when they yearned for a single drop of clean water? The injustice gnawed at him, a constant reminder that their suffering wasn't a natural disaster, but a man-made hell orchestrated by politicians and fueled by savagery.

Three vehicles clearly marked with the emblems of humanitarian aid organizations, making their way along a pre-arranged route coordinated with all parties involved, had been willfully struck by Israeli missiles. Seven aid workers—the very individuals devoted to easing the suffering of the afflicted—were now themselves the fallen casualties of this cowardly attack. Eight aid workers, angels who had flown into the inferno to ease suffering, were now casualties themselves. Bruno's breath hitched. He recognized their insignia, their mission—a grim reflection of his own. He'd crossed paths with them, exchanged weary nods of solidarity, a silent pact forged in the fires of war. One name pierced his heart—John. John, Ronnie's friend, Bruno's own tether to normalcy.

As Bruno watched the haunting footage, a sickening dread gripped him—the victims could easily have been him or any of the other humanitarian workers persisting in efforts to bring mercy to the innocents caught in the crossfire. Yet it was not him this time, but those beleaguered Palestinian civilians bearing the perpetual brunt of the senseless slaughter. When would this onslaught against the defenseless finally end? Bruno's heart, once filled with conviction, now felt hollowed by the cruelty of witnessing such wanton disregard for human life over and over again without reprieve.

Grief, a heavy weight in Bruno's chest, threatened to consume him. He felt the sting of tears behind his eyes, but they wouldn't fall. All he could manage was a choked sob, a guttural expression of the pain that clawed at his insides. He closed his eyes, images flashing behind his lids—faces, laughter, screams, and the ever present, suffocating dust of war. Each image was a story, a life shattered, a future stolen.

Back home, the sight of bustling streets and carefree laughter felt like a foreign land to Bruno. The luxury of safety, the normalcy he had taken for granted, now felt like a slap in the face. The weight of the atrocities he had witnessed, the resilience of those he left behind, pressed heavily on his soul.

Bruno knew this wasn't another mission trip to add to his deployment list. Rafah wasn't a war zone to be conquered, but a human story etched in blood and dust. The pain, the anger, the sheer helplessness—it settled on him like a suffocating fog. Yet, even in the darkest corners, flashes of defiance refused to be dimmed.

The medical teams in Palestine were a testament to unwavering resolve. They weren't warriors with guns, but warriors with stethoscopes and scalpels. With limited resources and under constant threat, they stood firm. Their days were a perpetual fight against injuries, illnesses, and the ever present fear of another attack. Yet, they never faltered. Each life saved, each bandage applied, was a defiant act against the destruction that surrounded them.

Then there were the journalists, risking their lives to become the voice of the voiceless. They weaved stories from the rubble, capturing the raw emotions of a people under siege. Their cameras were weapons of truth, their broadcasts a desperate plea to a world that seemed to be looking away. They documented the destruction, the resilience, the unyielding spirit of a population clinging to their land.

And the people themselves—the ones who refused to be uprooted. They remained witnesses to the enduring human spirit. Their homes were shattered, their lives uprooted, yet they held onto their land with a fierce pride. In their eyes burned a quiet fire—the unwavering belief that they would survive, that they would rebuild, that one day they would be free. This wasn't just a conflict; it was a fight for their very existence.

Bruno witnessed their struggle, their unwavering hope, and their defiance in the face of unimaginable hardship. It was these embers of humanity that ignited a spark within him, a glimmer of hope that refused to be extinguished. He may have been leaving Rafah, but Rafah, and the extraordinary spirit of its people, would forever hold a place within his heart.

This wasn't the end. It was a new beginning, a vow

etched onto Bruno's soul. He would return to Palestine, not as a soldier or an aid worker, but as a testament to the enduring spirit of humanity. He would return, not to fight a war, but to stand with those who refused to give up, to rebuild, to offer a sliver of hope in a world seemingly devoid of it. For in the depths of that war-torn city, Bruno had found a piece of himself he never knew existed, a fierce determination to fight for a world where the right to life wasn't a privilege, but a birthright.

10

The Weight of Hope

Witness to the Indomitable Spirit

I am Bruno. Perhaps you see a reflection of yourself in me —the one who refused to turn a blind eye to the suffering, the one who bore witness to the invincible strength of the human spirit rising from the ashes of destruction. But here's the raw, unvarnished truth: there are millions like you and me. Millions who, given the chance, would stand unwavering beside the broken and the beaten, who would fight with every fiber of their being for a world where the echoes of hope, not the thunder of bombs, resound through the streets. This isn't merely my story—it's a clarion call to action, a desperate plea for change. It's a soul shattering reminder that within each of us lies the power, the responsibility, to be the light the world so desperately needs in its darkest hour.

I am Bruno, and the stories on these pages are not mere fiction, but a heart-wrenching glimpse into the grim realityI witnessed during a mere three weeks amidst the grueling war that has ravaged Gaza for months on end.

Hope in the Rubble

The truth on the ground is far more brutal, more gut-wrenching than any words could ever hope to capture. Out of sheer necessity, I have altered names and omitted certain individuals and operations, a desperate attempt to shield the vulnerable and preserve the critical missions that offer a sign of hope in this unending nightmare. Even as these words find their way to you, the brutality continues to unfurl unabated, the suffering compounding with each passing day, each shattered life. What you hold in your hands is but a fragment, haunting proof of the staggering, unconscionable human toll of this merciless conflict. Though darkness may linger, an oppressive shroud that threatens to engulf us all, my hope, our hope, burns defiantly bright. These stories, tales of unimaginable resilience in the face of unspeakable horror, ignite a fire within me,Fueling my unyielding fight for a world where such atrocities are but a fading memory.

"THE HAVEN OF HOPE" remains a beacon of light, a critical sanctuary amidst the ceaseless maelstrom of conflict. By upholding the fundamental rights of every human being, particularly the most vulnerable among us—the children—the Haven ensures their safety, their dignity, and their access to the essential resources they so desperately need. In the face of such unmitigated brutality, no child should ever be reduced to a mere statistic, a nameless casualty in a war they never asked for. It is the solemn duty of the international community to come together, to support organizations like the Haven of Hope, and to fight tooth and nail for a future where every child has the chance to thrive, to dream, to live a life untainted by the scars of war. I remain unwavering in my commitment to the Haven of Hope, to the countless souls who have found shelter within its walls, and I will continue to lend my support, my voice, my very heart, in any way I can, for as long as it takes.

Earlier in the book, in chapter 7, when I mentioned "my gaze fell upon a raw, gaping wound in the earth near the hospital door," It turned out not to be a bomb crater. No, this was something far more chilling, a sight that haunts me to this day. Several weeks after I left Gaza, it was revealed on the news that it was a fresh mass grave, a hastily dug pit that served as a final resting place for the countless lives claimed by the relentless violence. I was shocked to find out it was a mass grave for the innocent civilians who had sought shelter within the hospital's walls, only to fall victim to the savage cruelty of the war. Even then, in that moment of gut-wrenching realization, I understood that this was but a horrifying premonition of the untold tragedies this war would continue to reveal in the years to come.

This makeshift cemetery, born of unrelenting violence, served as a haunting reminder of the true cost of war—a price paid in blood, tears, and shattered futures. Each life lost, each body laid to rest in this uncoremonious pit, represented a story brutally cut short, a family forever torn apart, and a future stolen.

The stench of death hung heavy in the air, a suffocating reminder of the staggering human toll of this conflict. I knew that the scars left by this war would run deep, that the true extent of the suffering would take years, if not decades, to fully unearth.

YET EVEN IN the face of such unspeakable horror, we must not let these lives be forgotten. It is our duty to bear witness to their tragic fates, to ensure that their stories are told, and to fight for a world where such atrocities become a distant memory.

Let this mass grave serve not as a symbol of hopelessness, but as a call to action—a reminder of the urgent need for peace, justice, and healing in a land ravaged by conflict. May we honor the memory of those laid to rest here by working tirelessly to build a future where no more innocent lives are lost to the senseless violence of war.

This year, an unsettling silence haunts the halls of Gaza's universities and schools. The jubilant celebrations of graduation, the culmination of years of dedicated study from primary school to doctoral programs, are conspicuously absent. The unceasing bombardment not only extinguishes the vibrant laughter and the hum of learning but also shatters the very foundation of hope for a brighter future.

This conflict is more than a mere war; it is a calculated assault on the aspirations and potential of an entire generation. The loss of educational institutions deals a crippling blow to the intellectual and cultural fabric of Gaza, robbing its youth of the opportunities they so desperately need to build a better tomorrow.

The silence that echoes through the empty classrooms and deserted campuses serves as a disturbing reminder of the incalculable human cost of this war—a price paid not just in lives lost but in dreams deferred and futures derailed. It is a tragic validation of the far-reaching consequences of violence, a grim portrait of a society stripped of its most precious resource: the minds and hearts of its young people.

That experience is a crucible that simultaneously shatters and rebuilds me. It strips away the layers of indifference and the petty worries that once consumed my thoughts. The daily anxieties that seem so monumental back home—the traffic jams, the burned toast, the missed promotions—all pale in comparison to the raw, desperate struggle for survival I witnessed every single day.

In the comfort of our daily lives, we often take for granted the most basic necessities. Clean water, shelter, and the freedom to walk the streets without fear are fundamental rights that tragically become luxuries in war zones. There, life is reduced to a brutal lottery, where survival hinges on an unfair roll of the dice. This harsh realization forces us to adopt a more grounded perspective on our own lives. The anxieties and trivial matters that consume us might be unimaginable dreams for those fighting for basic necessities amidst the chaos of war.

Injustice undeniably marks the global stage, with the recent conflict in Palestine serving as a stark reminder. However, this harsh reality is replicated in countless corners of the world. Tragically, it often takes the brutality of war and devastating loss for this truth to fully resonate. Children become orphans overnight, families are torn apart, and aspirations are extinguished in the blink of an eye. In the face of such suffering, personal grief and sorrow are put on hold.

The chasm between their plight and the comfort we enjoy in our daily lives is undeniable. However, this disparity should not be a source of despair; rather, it should ignite a call to action. Leveraging our voices and skills to champion humanity and the fundamental rights of all people, regardless of ethnicity, religion, or background, is not a burden but a responsibility. This message resonates with aid workers across the globe and should resonate with every citizen of the world.

The world feels like it's crumbling beneath our feet, a seismic upheaval of despair and anguish. The harrowing images from Palestine sear themselves into our collective consciousness—innocent children, eyes wide with primal terror, clinging desperately to the tattered remnants of their shattered lives. Once vibrant families, tapestries woven with love and laughter, now lie in tatters, their dreams scattered like ashes on the unforgiving winds of war. Cruel, merciless hands snatch away loved ones, leaving behind a yawning chasm of grief, an abyss echoing with unanswered questions and stifled sobs. In this grueling struggle for survival, there's no respite for sorrow, no sanctuary for the heart's lament.

An ocean of privilege and comfort separates us from their fathomless despair. We slumber beneath tranquil skies, oblivious to the cacophonous symphony of bombs that rends their nights asunder. This distance, this disparity, feels like a bitter betrayal, a stark reminder of the immense advantages we clutch so carelessly. Yet amidst the suffocating weight of sadness, an inextinguishable ember of hope ignites.

WE POSSESS the power to bridge this gaping chasm, not with the callous indifference of apathy, but with the profound, transformative force of empathy. Our voices, raised in unison, can shake the very foundations of silence, shattering the walls of indifference. Our skills, no matter how humble, can become potent instruments of change, catalysts for a world to be reborn. This is no mere burden—it is a spark rising from the depths of human suffering, a desperate plea for action. Let the searing pain we witness become the fuel that propels us forward, the driving force behind our unwavering commitment to justice. Let the world resound with the thunderous chorus of our outrage, a defiant melody demanding the birth of a new era—an age where every child can once again dare to dream, unshackled by the fetters of fear.

This struggle transcends the borders of Palestine; it reverberates in every war-ravaged corner of our fractured globe. It speaks to the universality of human anguish, the common thread of grief that binds us all, regardless of creed or culture. We must rise above the clamor of discord, not with the caustic fury of anger, but with a profound, soul-stirring sadness that compels us to act, to be the change we so desperately seek.

Palestine was more than a mere war zone; it was a crucible of the human spirit, forging an indelible reminder of humanity's unfinished quest for equality, freedom, and justice in every corner of our shared world. These are no distant, abstract dreams—they are the very foundation upon which we must build a future where no child trembles beneath the shadow of bomb laden skies. Brick by agonizing brick, we must labor to construct this brave new world, to relegate such unfathomable tragedies to the darkest annals of history, mere echoes of a bygone era that shall never again darken our collective horizon.

The faces I encountered in Gaza are forever etched into the very fabric of my being—their luminous eyes, their radiant smiles, their heart-wrenching tears, and their unforgettable names indelibly seared into the depths of my memory. The unimaginable pain they endured, the unspeakable horrors they witnessed, are a testament to the indomitable strength of the human spirit. Yet even amidst the wreckage of their lives, they cling to the dream of peace, to the fervent hope for a brighter tomorrow. In their resilient smiles, I see echoes of the same inextinguishable hope that shines in the eyes of the oppressed and the marginalized across the globe—a universal longing for a world made whole.

Hope in the Rubble

Their courageous struggle serves as a call to action, a poignant reminder of our shared responsibility to uplift the downtrodden, to be a voice for the voiceless, to champion the inalienable rights of every human being. We must stand as unwavering allies to those who have been cast aside, relegated to the margins of society, denied the basic dignities that should be the birthright of all. In the face of injustice, we must rise as a united front, our voices melding into a thunderous chorus that demands change, which refuses to be silenced until every soul is granted the sacred right to live, to thrive, to dream.

Though the challenges they face may seem insurmountable, though the darkness that engulfs them may appear impenetrable, the indomitable spirit of the people of Gaza shines like a sign of hope amidst the ruins. In their ability to find light in the bleakest of shadows, to nurture the seeds of joy in the most barren of soils, I find a wellspring of inspiration that knows no bounds. Their laughter, ringing out defiantly against the cacophony of war, is evidence of the resilience of the human heart, a powerful reminder that even in the face of unimaginable adversity, the flame of hope can never be fully extinguished.

As we bear witness to their stories, as we allow their struggles to sear themselves into our consciousness, we must let their anguish ignite a fierce and unrelenting determination within us. We must become the champions of the oppressed, the guardians of dignity, the defenders of the basic human rights that should be the inalienable possession of every man, woman, and child on this Earth. In the face of injustice, silence is complicity; inaction is a betrayal of our shared humanity. We must rise, we must speak, we must act—not with empty platitudes, but with concrete deeds that shatter the chains of oppression and pave the way for a world reborn.

In the resilient smiles of the people of Gaza, I see a reflection of the universal human spirit—a spirit that refuses to be broken, that dares to dream of a better tomorrow even as the nightmares of today threaten to consume it all. Though their individual stories may one day fade from the public eye, though the specifics of their struggles may be lost to the relentless march of time, the invincible essence of their spirit must forever serve as a guiding light for us all. It must be the driving force that propels us forward, that fuels our unwavering commitment to building a world where justice reigns supreme, where equality is not a lofty ideal but a lived reality, where every human being is granted the dignity and respect they so richly deserve.

The world may be broken, fractured along the fault lines of injustice and oppression, but I, Bruno, refuse to surrender to despair. I will not let the darkness extinguish the flame of hope that burns within me, the unquenchable fire that drives me to be an agent of change, a beacon of light in a world too often shrouded in shadow.

I am Bruno, and this is my solemn vow, my sacred promise to the people of Gaza and to all those who suffer under the yoke of injustice: I will never forget. I will carry your stories etched upon my heart, a constant reminder of the work that lies ahead. My voice will rise against the forces of oppression, a thunderous denunciation of the structures that perpetuate inequality and suffering. My hands will reach out, a lifeline to those in need, a symbol of the unbreakable bonds of human solidarity that transcends all borders and barriers. And my spirit, forged in the crucible of your struggles, will never falter, never waver in the face of adversity. I will march forward, a relentless warrior in the battle for a brighter tomorrow, a world where every child can wake to a dawn of limitless possibility.

I will never stop helping, never stop fighting, never stop believing in the power of compassion to transform even the darkest of realities. I will stand with you, shoulder to shoulder, heart to heart, until the day when justice rolls down like waters and righteousness like a mighty stream. Together, we will build a world where love triumphs over hatred, where empathy vanquishes apathy, where the light of hope forever banishes the darkness of despair.

This is my promise, my sacred duty, my unwavering commitment to you and to all those who dream of a better tomorrow. In solidarity, in strength, in the unshakable conviction that a brighter future is not only possible but inevitable, I stand with you. Always.

Afterword

As I pen these final words, my thoughts are drawn back to the faces etched into my memory—the children, women, and men whose lives have been forever altered by the relentless tides of war. Their stories, their resilience in the face of unimaginable adversity, serve as a poignant reminder that we are all interconnected, that the pain and suffering of one is the pain and suffering of us all.

In a world that often feels fractured and divided, it is more important than ever to remember that we do not walk this path alone. We share this Earth, this precious blue marble suspended in the vastness of space, with countless others—each with their own hopes, dreams, and fears.

It is my fervent hope that the stories contained within these pages will serve as a catalyst for change, a spark that ignites the flames of compassion and understanding in the hearts of all who read them. For it is only through empathy, through the recognition of our shared humanity, that we can begin to build bridges across the chasms that divide us.

Afterword

Peace, lasting and true, is not an unattainable dream. It is a goal that we must work towards every day, with every action, no matter how small. Each of us, in our own unique way, has the power to make a difference. Whether through our words, our deeds, or the simple act of bearing witness to the stories of others, we all have a role to play in shaping a better tomorrow.

As the tragedy in Gaza continues to unfold, as more and more children lose their lives and families are forced to flee in search of safety and basic human needs, we must not allow ourselves to become numb to their suffering. We must continue to stand in solidarity with those who have lost so much, to lend our voices to the call for justice and peace.

The road ahead may be long and uncertain, but I firmly believe that by working together, by harnessing the power of our collective compassion and determination, we can create a world where the horrors of war are relegated to the pages of history, where every child can grow up free from fear, and where every human being is treated with the dignity and respect they deserve.

As we close this chapter and begin the next, let us carry the stories of those we have met here in our hearts. Let us honor their sacrifices by dedicating ourselves to the pursuit of peace, not just in Gaza, but in every corner of this precious world we call home.

We will meet again. Until then, let us hold fast to the power of hope, the strength of our shared humanity, and the unwavering belief that a better world is possible.

With love and solidarity,
Bruno

www.ingramcontent.com/pod-product-compliance
Lightning Source LLC
Chambersburg PA
CBHW070432010526
44118CB00014B/2008